LEAD LIKE A WOMAN

Grateful
Volume 1

**Brought to you by Andrea Heuston
Featuring 11 Grateful
Female Leaders**

Lead Like a Woman: Grateful

Copyright © 2025 by Andrea Heuston, Lead Like a Woman Press.

All rights reserved. No part of this publication may be reproduced, distributed or transmitted in any form or by any means, including photocopying, recording, or other electronic or mechanical methods, without the prior written permission of the publisher, except in the case of brief quotations embodied in critical reviews and certain other noncommercial uses permitted by copyright law.

This book is for entertainment and education purposes only. It is not intended to serve as business or life advice. This book is not intended to instruct or advise in any way. Using any of the information in this book is based on the reader's own judgment after consulting with his or her trusted professionals. The views expressed herein are not necessarily those of the publisher, nor the other co-authors.

Published by Prominence Publishing

www.Prominencepublishing.com

ISBN: 978-1-990830-81-5

Dedicated to Dr. Kristin Kahle's Mother,
Laura E. Kahle,
August 16, 1945 – December 25th, 2024

"I am grateful for the strength she has given me. I am sure that I would not be the same woman I am without her."

Table of Contents

FOREWORD By Helena Gibson 1

INTRODUCTION 3

CHAPTER 1: Finding Gratitude in Fire
By Andrea Heuston 9

CHAPTER 2: The Heart of Gratitude:
Lessons in Love, Loss, and Growth
By Fran Biderman-Gross 25

CHAPTER 3: Gratitude for My Mother
By Dr. Kristin L Kahle 41

CHAPTER 4: The Golden Glue: An Essay on Gratitude
By Effie Bar-Caspi 55

CHAPTER 5: Gratitude And…
By Shenandoah Davis 67

CHAPTER 6: Finding Grace 83
By Adrienne Palmer 83

CHAPTER 7 Forged in Fire
By Marsha Ralls 103

TABLE OF CONTENTS

CHAPTER 8: The Power of Gratitude:
A Journey of Empowerment and Transformation
By Manon de Veritch 121

CHAPTER 9: Gratitude & Grace
By Amy Boone Thompson 139

CHAPTER 10: From Chaos to Calm: A Gratitude Journey
By Daniella Menachemson 149

CHAPTER 11: Two Sides of Gratitude
(Or, Learning to Love My Critter Brain)
By Cheryl Farr 165

EPILOGUE 187

BOOK CLUB QUESTIONS 190

Foreword

By Helena Gibson

WHEN MY DEAR FRIEND ANDREA HEUSTON asked me to write a foreword for her latest book in the "Lead Like a Woman" series focused on gratitude, the answer was simple. Gratitude—for our friendship, for the memories we've shared, and for this opportunity to support a woman who inspires so many—was my guiding emotion.

To me, gratitude is a fundamental principle for those who dare to lead and transform lives. When woven into leadership, it nurtures resilience, fuels meaningful connections, and empowers every interaction, propelling us all toward greater heights.

Throughout my journey as the founder of Strut Hair Solutions and Unveil Hair Care, gratitude has consistently illuminated my path—from moments of struggle to though the successes. It has been a grounding force during challenges, such as expanding my businesses amid global crises, supporting cancer

FOREWORD

patients on their unique journeys, and advocating for all women dealing with hair loss. In each experience, gratitude has deepened my purpose.

In this book, Andrea and the authors explore how gratitude shapes not only professional achievements but also the hearts and souls of women who lead with grace and fortitude. The stories within reflect lives driven by compassion, generosity, and a dedication to uplifting others.

I invite you to read, reflect, and allow these lessons of gratitude to move you. Share your own reflections with the women in your life, and together, let's celebrate the strength and light created when gratitude leads the way.

Helena Gibson,
Founder, Strut Hair Solutions and Unveil Hair Care

Introduction

"Gratitude is said to be the memory of the heart."
—Jean-Baptiste Massieu

Dear Reader,

I'M SO EXCITED YOU'VE JOINED US. This is the fourth book in the *Lead Like a Woman* series. The series has gained momentum: more incredible female authors, stories of leadership through the stormy times, and greater traction with our message. I'm excited to present you with *Lead Like a Woman: GRATEFUL* in two volumes.

The quality of being grateful has been studied by researchers for the last twenty years. How does being grateful impact mental health? Research shows it can reduce stress and improve physical and mental health. "...many studies over the past decade have found that people who consciously count their blessings tend to be happier and less depressed...." Learn more from *Gratitude Changes You And Your Brain* (Berkeley's *Greater Good* Magazine).

INTRODUCTION

But gratitude isn't just about counting blessings when life is smooth—it's about finding meaning and growth in our greatest challenges. My own journey with gratitude has taught me this profound truth in ways I never expected.

I am grateful for five years of infertility treatments. Yes, grateful. Those years of uncertainty and hope brought my husband and me closer than we'd ever been, teaching us resilience and partnership in ways that prepared us for an even greater blessing: adopting our two beautiful boys at birth, both from the same birth mother. What seemed like endless waiting became the perfect preparation for the family we were meant to have.

I am grateful for having been in a coma. In that darkness came clarity—the realization that I didn't have to do it all, that taking control of my health wasn't optional but essential. And I have! That experience became a catalyst for transformation, teaching me to prioritize what truly matters and to take care of myself with the same dedication I give to others.

I am grateful for watching our house burn down. In the ashes of material possessions, we discovered what can never be destroyed: the strength of family, the support of community, and the resilience of the human spirit. From that devastation came renewal, teaching us that home isn't about walls and roofs—it's about the love we share and the memories we create.

I am grateful for grief. In its heavy depths, grief has taught me about the profound capacity of the human heart—how it can hurt deeply because it has loved deeply, and how that very pain connects us to the essence of being alive and to others who understand loss.

And yes, I am grateful for the small moments that make life beautiful: the burst of flavor in a fresh strawberry, the delicate patterns of frost on autumn leaves, the comforting warmth of a fire in the fireplace, the aroma of homemade bread filling the kitchen. These simple pleasures remind us that gratitude isn't reserved for grand moments—it's found in the ordinary magic of everyday life.

Through these experiences, I've learned that gratitude isn't just a feel-good practice—it's a transformative force that shapes how we lead, how we love, and how we live. It's about finding meaning in both the triumphs and the trials, understanding that

INTRODUCTION

every experience, even the painful ones, carries within it the seeds of growth and wisdom.

In this collection, you'll find stories from remarkable women who have discovered their own paths to grateful leadership. Their experiences, while unique, share a common thread: the understanding that gratitude isn't just about saying "thank you" when things go well. It's about maintaining perspective in challenges, finding strength in vulnerability, and leading with an open heart that recognizes the value in every experience.

As you read these pages, I invite you to reflect on your own journey with gratitude. What challenges have shaped you? What unexpected blessings have emerged from difficult times? How has gratitude influenced your leadership style and your relationships?

Together, let's explore how grateful leadership can transform not just our professional lives, but our entire approach to living and leading. The enthusiasm for this project brought together twenty-two remarkable women leaders, each with powerful insights about grateful leadership. To best share their wisdom, we've presented their stories in two companion volumes. Each volume contains eleven chapters exploring different facets of leading with gratitude, offering diverse perspectives and experiences that illuminate the transformative power of grateful leadership.

Whether you begin with Volume 1 or Volume 2, you'll find stories that inspire, challenge, and encourage you to explore your own relationship with grateful leadership. I encourage you to read both volumes to experience the full richness of insights our twenty-two authors bring to this exploration of gratitude in leadership.

Welcome to a journey of discovery, growth, and profound appreciation for all that life brings our way.

With deepest gratitude,
Andrea Heuston

CHAPTER 1

Finding Gratitude in Fire

> *"She wore her scars as her best attire.*
> *A stunning dress made of hellfire."*
> —Daniel Saint

By Andrea Heuston

August 4, 2014

THE BOYS AND I HAD JUST STARTED our annual month-long stay at the beach house. This was back before they were young adults with their own lives who say things like, "Nope, not spending a month with mom in a remote place. Sorry." But back then, they loved it.

We'd play on the beach all day, challenging ourselves to see how long we could go without getting in the car for anything.

FINDING GRATITUDE IN FIRE

The house was about three miles from town, so we'd ride bikes to get groceries and do whatever we could to avoid driving. Those summers were always my favorite time of the year—a chance to connect with my family distanced from the pressures of the outside world. The beach house was my haven, my little castle.

August 4th had been a beautiful sunny day of adventures. After dinner, the boys and I decided to take a walk down the road. We were in shorts, and quickly got chilly as we felt the fog rolling in. Hurrying back, I put a fire in the fireplace to warm up the house before tucking the boys into bed.

About 20 minutes later, I heard an alarming noise, like a jet landing on the roof. I ran outside to investigate just as someone started honking in my driveway. He yelled, "You have a chimney fire!" Rushing back inside, I doused the fireplace flames with a pitcher of water. But when I walked down the trail and saw fire spreading on the roof, I knew our lives were about to change.

Making the frantic call to 911, I raced upstairs to wake up Aidan and Owen, who were sleeping soundly in the top bunks. "The roof is on fire!" I yelled, urging them to throw on clothes and get outside. Across the street, In our neighbor's driveway, we stood crying in the flashing red lights as the beautiful house that was our sanctuary filled with flames. Firefighters poured in from three different departments as the blaze grew to five alarms. That night, we lost our physical home, but in the fear and devastation, I found something I didn't expect—a seed of gratitude that we were together and unharmed.

As I watched the flames devour the roof, my mind flashed back to tucking the boys into those top bunks mere hours ago. A wave of nausea hit me as I realized how differently this night could have ended if the fire had started after we were asleep, if we hadn't heard the alarms, or if the ceiling had given way sooner. Hugging my sons tight as the inferno raged, I repeated a mantra over and over in my head—"We're okay, we're okay, we're okay"—as if I could make it more true with each fierce iteration. Tears and ash mingled on my face as the magnitude of it all crashed over me in relentless waves—the terror of what could have been and the knee-buckling relief that we had escaped with our lives. I knew this earth-shattering event would be a defining "before and after" moment for our family. But we were here, and we were whole. Everything else was just stuff.

When the chaos died down, and it was clear the house was a total loss, a police officer helped us navigate our next steps. He called a nephew who worked at a nearby hotel and arranged a room for us since we had no means to pay with my purse still in the burning house. I felt dazed with shock and overwhelmed but also so profoundly grateful for the instant support and compassion cushioning the worst night of our lives.

Sometime in the surreal pre-dawn hours, as the boys fitfully dozed and my mind spun in a million directions, I picked up my phone. It was the end of a 30-day gratitude challenge I'd been participating in on Facebook. My finger hovered over the screen, wondering what to possibly say. I settled on raw honesty, sharing the bare facts of the massive loss but ending with appreciation for the safety of my little family, the incredible first responders, and the community already rallying around us. It was a tiny light in the darkness, a reminder to my shattered heart to keep looking for the good, even now.

The Aftermath

We woke the next morning to discover the world hadn't stopped turning and that people are amazing. As word spread about our situation, a network of love instantly mobilized. Dear friends left their house at 5:00 am to be by our side, arriving with bags of clothes, toiletries, snacks, and most importantly, hugs and listening ears. Neighbors we barely knew opened their homes to us without hesitation. The insurance company handed us a substantial check to start putting the pieces back together. The boys' prized iPads were even miraculously found intact under fallen debris. Everywhere we turned, in the midst of senseless loss, care and compassion surrounded us.

I kept waiting to wake up from this surreal nightmare. Walking through the hollowed-out remains of our beach house for the first time was a sucker punch to the soul. Charred timbers and puddles of ashy water had replaced cozy rooms that used to be filled with love and laughter. It hurt to tell the boys that their room had been destroyed, and the beds they'd been peacefully sleeping in hours before were now gone. Yet, in the same breath, I could look at their sweet faces and marvel with knee-buckling relief that the ceiling had not given way until after they were safe outside. We'd lost a place that had felt like an extension of ourselves, but we were still wholly us—a little shaken and smelling of smoke (which lasted for days and through countless showers), but together and strong.

Over the next few days and weeks, I ricocheted wildly between gratitude and grief. One moment, I'd be in tears over a half-burned photo album; the next, overwhelmed with emotion at the generosity of a kind word or deed. The constant influx of insurance calls, paperwork, and decisions pressed on me. I longed for the simplicity of our beach days, now seeming like something from another lifetime. But every hard minute was tempered by a deep sense of perspective. All the stress and hassle was in service of rebuilding our lives—lives we got to continue living. What a gift to have this chance.

And oh, there were so many gifts. Our neighbor opened up his vacant rental house for us to stay in indefinitely. A local builder offered his services to start drawing up plans free of charge. Family, friends, even strangers sent emails and cards full of encouragement and donations. Watching my community materialize around me, showing up to help us carry this hardship, flooded me with something beyond gratitude—a restored sense of faith in humanity, in the fundamental goodness of people. Our lives had literally gone up in flames, but I'd never felt more supported or loved.

In the middle of this outpouring, a deeper truth began to settle into my bones. For so long, the beach house had been my anchor, the place I'd attached so much of my identity and happiness to. I genuinely believed my family needed that specific set of walls to connect, that I needed that patch of sand to feel like myself. The fire forced me to confront the question: *Who am I when the external trappings are stripped away?* It was disorienting and painful and utterly necessary, shaking me out of my clinging to a certain circumstance for my wholeness.

I began to understand that while that house had absolutely fostered so much joyful bonding and growth, the essence of what made it special had always lived in us, not the building. The structure burning down couldn't erase the love, the memories, and the resilient spirit we'd nurtured there. If anything, it was distilling us down to what mattered most. This experience was an invitation to shift my perspective from outer to inner, to put down roots in my own heart instead of four walls. Slowly, stubbornly, I started to heal and rebuild from the inside out.

Rebuilding

Of course, we had to literally rebuild, too, and that process was its own journey of fire. I thought I'd gained some acceptance and perspective from the initial loss, armed with my fledging gratitude practice and determination to focus on the positive. Then we started construction, and my calm veneer began to crack under the stress.

I threw myself into the role of project manager, obsessively trying to will the new house into existence through sheer force of effort. When our builder's initial promise of being done in six months stretched to a year filled with delays and red tape, I felt my hard-won appreciation faltering. Insurance assessments, material costs, building codes, loan payouts, all the details I desperately tried to control so we could just get back home—I watched them slip through my fingers over and over and over again.

There were many days I fell into a dark, emotional place, lashing out at our contractor and feeling angry and disconnected from myself. I grieved intensely for the beach house as it was before, this special haven that I'd come to believe was the only place I could truly be 'me.' Without that anchor of identity, I felt lost and untethered. The illusion of control I'd wrapped around our family's sanctuary going up in flames forced me to confront some hard truths.

As the months dragged on and my frustration mounted, I had a poignant realization. In all my laser focus on the end goal, I was missing the sacredness of the process. Just like the night of the fire, when I'd woken up to what mattered most, I needed to zoom out and shift my perspective. Yes, rebuilding a house that was so precious to us was important and consuming work. But in many ways, the real reconstruction was happening within myself and my family.

With intentional effort, I started to unclench my metaphorical fists. I apologized to our builder, who was truly doing his best. I voiced more appreciation to the boys, who were being so resilient. I took it day by day, celebrating small victories and milestones instead of fretting about the timeline. Slowly, as I let go of my death grip on the external circumstances, I felt a deeper peace welling up. Our home wasn't done yet, but we were going to be okay. We already were.

The day that it hit me the hardest, and the day that I felt the most grief, was at the end of December that year. We'd been staying at a house up the coast, and it had been five months since the fire. We had a new puppy named Lola, and my beloved Grandma Gerry had just died. It was a gray, rainy, wet, nasty day, as often happens on the Washington coast during the winter. We drove down to the house because we wanted to see the progress and learned there was no progress. There were no walls. There were no floors. It was all two-by-fours, and water was pouring in through the roof.

I sat down on the wet floor with the rain soaking into me and cried my eyes out. That's when the bottom dropped out. I had cried before, I had talked about it, but I hadn't really felt it. That was the day I began to let the emotion out. It was another one of those moments I'll remember forever. It's the day I began the healing process.

Two months later, as I stood shivering in the bare skeleton of a living room, instead of spiraling down into sorrow, I took a deep breath. I looked out at the angry ocean through glassless windows, its turbulence a mirror of my own roiling emotions. Closing my eyes, I conjured up a vivid reel of moments from the past—laughter over dance parties in the living room, cozy movie nights curled up together, salty hair and happy faces after long beach days. I let those golden memories wash over me, feeling them fully, honoring their preciousness. And then I took another breath and gently released them.

Because we weren't moving backwards, no matter how much I wished we could sometimes. This house would never be exactly the same as before the fire. *We* would never be exactly the same. The only way was forward, into a new story—one that included this momentous plot twist of the fire but wasn't singularly defined by it. One that carried the essence and love of what came before but distilled down and stronger, the extraneous stuff burnt away. I could keep looking at this new house like a poor imitation...or I could choose to see it as a chance to expand, to be reborn even better.

I opened my eyes, blinking away tears. The rain was clearing, hints of blue peeking through. Shafts of light streamed across the plywood floor, limning tools, and beams. The space felt different to me then—not empty, but full of possibility. For the first time, I could feel the love waiting to fill these walls, the future memories ready to take root. I could sense the same resilient spirit that had always been the real magic of the beach house, hovering and ready to alight in this new space. My heart lifted, cautiously hopeful.

I understood then that this whole process—the fire, the grief, the rebuilding—it wasn't a test to endure but an opportunity to grow. To learn that my true sanctuary isn't a place but a peace inside myself. To live into the truth that a family's foundation isn't poured from concrete, but from how we show up for each other, in good times and bad. To prove to myself that I can walk through the flames and come out the other side—not unscathed, but stronger in all the places that matter most.

In that unfinished living room, I made a vow. To keep choosing gratitude and grace over grasping for control. To trust the journey of rebuilding, both inside and out. To let this new house be not just a replica of what we lost but a testament to what we'd overcome together. To fill it not with stuff, but with the kind of presence, appreciation and love that can never be lost. That day, as I walked back out into the weak sunlight, I felt something new rising up alongside those bare walls—a profound sense of peace, of purpose. Of coming home to myself.

Stronger on the Other Side of Fire

Our rebuilt beach house is a phoenix, a stunning testament to fortitude and the incredible power of community and hope in the face of heartbreak. Now, when I walk through the door, I'm overwhelmed with gratitude not just for the comforting embrace of the walls around me but for the transformation they represent. The new rooms are a manifestation of our own family's journey through the flames and out the other side. We've all been refined, distilled down to what matters most, and rebuilt with a sturdier foundation.

I've learned that while we aren't defined by the hard things that happen to us, we are absolutely shaped by them. The sacred process of rising from the ashes of tragedy has taught me that I can't control the literal or metaphorical storms that blow through our lives. I know now that no amount of worry or resistance will stop difficult things from happening. Suffering is an unavoidable part of the human experience.

But I can choose how I respond when the ground falls out from under me. I get to decide where to focus my energy—on lamenting what I've lost or leaning into appreciating what remains. This experience has shown me that if I look close enough, even in the darkest times, there are always embers of grace and spots of light to be found and fanned. Letting go of the illusion of control, owning my reactions, and choosing to trust that I am built from strong enough stuff to withstand hard times have been the greatest unexpected gifts of this journey.

In the end, I'm grateful for my relationship with fire. For how it burned away my attachment to false security outside myself. For illuminating what matters most when everything else falls away. For showing me that real roots are not anchored in any one place but in the infinite love and connection we nurture in our hearts. For teaching me to find beauty, meaning, and growth in the ashes.

If the worst happens and your life goes up in flames, know that it's not the end of your story. You will feel the full intensity and heat of the grief, and it will hurt like hell. But if you can muster up the courage to pick through the rubble and look a little closer, you just might find some incredible embers of strength, gratitude, and grace buried in there, too, smoldering and ready to ignite something exquisite.

About the Author

Andrea Heuston, the dynamic CEO of Artitudes and the force behind the Lead Like a Woman Movement, brings her vibrant personality, creative expertise, and speaker coaching skills to every endeavor. With a passion for communication and a knack for captivating audiences, she transforms ordinary presentations into extraordinary experiences. As a successful entrepreneur, Andrea understands the unique challenges faced by female business leaders.

With over 30 years of experience in the tech industry, Andrea started "The Lead Like a Woman Show" podcast in 2020. The show charts internationally on a weekly basis and has over 40,000 followers on social media. The Lead Like a Woman Show focuses on empowering female leaders to empower others through topical discussions and interviews.

Andrea is passionate about helping to close the gender gap for women in business and she has a goal to help 1 million women own their stage by April of 2031.

Connect with Andrea:

http://AndreaHeuston.com

http://Leadlikeawoman.biz

https://www.linkedin.com/in/andreaheuston/

#LeadLikeAWoman

CHAPTER 2

The Heart of Gratitude: Lessons in Love, Loss, and Growth

"Where there's a will, there's always a way."

By Fran Biderman-Gross

LIFE HAS NEVER BEEN SIMPLE, and I wouldn't want it to be. Each setback and victory shaped who I am. Those moments of uncertainty may feel insurmountable at the time, but when I look back, I see how each one pushed me to grow, adapt, and rise above. It's a process of continuous transformation, experiences that shaped me into who I am today.

Yet, I've learned that gratitude isn't just a passive emotion; it's an active choice, a lens through which all those experiences gain new meaning. Instead of dwelling on the hardships, I choose to see the lessons they carry. This shift in perspective has turned trials into turning points and doubts into deeper understanding. In hindsight, what once seemed overwhelming now stands as proof of resilience and hope.

Always Becoming: Embrace the Journey

It was a quiet moment—one of those rare instances when the clamor of the world seemed to still. My mentor looked at me, eyes filled with both kindness and conviction, and said, "You are in a state of becoming." Six simple words, but they landed like a thunderclap, reminding me that life unfolds in small, meaningful moments. Instead, it's about giving ourselves permission to fall short, learn, and rise again. Suddenly, I realized how much there was to be grateful for in the messy, beautiful process of growth. Every misstep, every stumble, became a steppingstone rather than a dead end, and with each one, I found new strength I hadn't known was there. "Becoming" set me free from the need to be perfect and opened my eyes to how each experience—good or bad—carves out a deeper capacity for gratitude.

Stay Present: Find Gratitude in the Here and Now

Another mentor offered a lesson just as transformative: "Stay present." At first, it sounded like simple advice, but over time I discovered and harnessed its extreme power. When our minds drift into worries about what might be or regrets about what was, we lose sight of the opportunities unfolding right in front of us. Anchoring ourselves in the present moment means dealing with *what is* rather than *what if,* and with that shift, gratitude comes more naturally. We begin to notice the small blessings—a conversation that sparks new ideas, the warmth of a loved one's smile, the calming hush of early morning. Each time I feel my mind begin to spiral into future fears or past regrets, I pause, take a breath, and come back to *now - to stay present*. In doing so, I reclaim my focus and my sense of peace, recognizing the simple truth that gratitude thrives in the reality of the moment, not in the shadows of our imagination.

Still, even with this perspective, one truth remains clear: I have never walked this path alone. I've been shaped by the guiding hands of family, mentors, and friends—each leaving an indelible mark on my story. Their lessons, love, and, at times, challenges have been the steady force molding my character. They

THE HEART OF GRATITUDE: LESSONS IN LOVE, LOSS, AND GROWTH

remind me that we're never truly on our own—when we fall, there's a hand to catch us; when we question, there's a voice that offers wisdom; and when we triumph, there's a heart that celebrates along with us.

The reflections I share here are a tribute to these remarkable influences and their infinite wisdom. Their impact resonates in every choice I make and every goal I pursue, fueling my commitment to live with gratitude, no matter how winding the road may be. In sharing their stories—and the ways they shaped me—I hope to offer inspiration for anyone who's ever felt tested by life, only to discover that it was in those very challenges that true growth began.

My Mother: A Beacon of Strength

This year, I lost my mother after a six-year battle with ovarian cancer—a fight that was heartbreaking to witness but also revealed her remarkable resilience and love. She wasn't just my mother; she was my compass and my anchor, always guiding me with quiet determination and a boundless appetite for understanding life at its very core.

Her hands were rarely still. They were always creating—crafting, building, nurturing—and she poured her energy into our family, turning struggles into lessons. One summer, she decided to grow carrots and green beans in every color she could find—not just orange and green, but purple, yellow, and everything in between. With a scientist's curiosity, she tracked how they grew, tasted, and responded to different conditions. To the rest of us, it sometimes felt extreme, but for her, it was about getting to the root: How do things work? Why do they differ? What can we learn by paying attention?

That spirit of inquiry went far beyond the garden. "Stand tall," she'd often tell me, "Even when the world tries to shrink you." Those words, I now realize, mirrored her approach to living. Whether experimenting with vegetables or facing down a relentless disease, she believed in digging deeper—seeking truth, embracing challenges, and trusting that growth comes from persistence.

In her final months, we shared conversations I'll carry with me forever. Even as her strength waned, she refused to let cancer define her. Instead, she showed me the power of grace and honesty in the face of pain. The love she poured into me from childhood onward became my bedrock. Now, whenever I'm tempted to give up or shy away from a challenge, I feel her quiet strength guiding me. She taught me that true resilience is rooted in curiosity, courage, and love.

Grandma Ruth: Perfectionism and Love

Grandma Ruth was a stickler—a perfectionist to her core. Her expectations for her family were impossibly high, and as a child, it was easy to feel like I wasn't measuring up. Yet, in her kitchen, everything changed. Cooking was her love language, and her kitchen was her haven.

I knew the holidays had truly arrived the moment Grandma walked in the door—her presence instantly filling the house with warmth and the promise of great food. She would visit days in advance to start cooking, and I'd countdown to her arrival like a child waiting for a favorite relative. I'd wake up early, practically buzzing with anticipation. Of course, nothing began before Grandma's coffee and cottage cheese, but as soon as she was ready, I'd be at the fridge, pulling out ingredients for her mental "to-cook" list. She never wrote it down; instead, she carried each dish in her head like a perfectly orchestrated symphony. "Start with the right ingredients," she'd say, "it is the only way to ensure a proper outcome."

As the oldest granddaughter, I became her sous chef, standing by her side as she meticulously prepared everything from slow-braised meats to hearty soups. The aroma that filled our kitchen was as comforting as a warm hug—onions sizzling, spices mingling, soup simmering. It was in the midst of that delicious chaos that I saw the softer side of Grandma Ruth. Her laughter would echo through the house, her stories—vivid and often humorous—offering glimpses into the life she had lived before becoming "Grandma."

Her hands, firm and practiced, guided mine as I learned to chop, stir, and coax flavors from simple ingredients. In those moments, I understood her perfectionism was never about harsh criticism; it was about love—a desire to bring out the best in the people she cared for. To this day, whenever I step into my own kitchen, I think of her. Her recipes continue to nourish my family, and her lessons—on precision, hard work, and the deeper joy of nurturing others—remain a lasting tradition.

THE HEART OF GRATITUDE: LESSONS IN LOVE, LOSS, AND GROWTH

My Father: A Model of Perseverance

My father, Bernie, was a remarkable man. He lost his father to a sudden heart attack at just 19 and his mother to a stroke a few years later. Navigating life without the guidance of loving parents is a monumental challenge, yet he persevered with unshakable strength and determination. He built a successful career, became a respected leader in his community, and—most importantly—created a family defined by love and support.

His lessons came not in grand speeches but through his quiet, steady example. "Do what's right, not what's easy," he'd say, and these simple words became my compass. I saw that motto in action when our community needed a new synagogue. Despite skepticism and countless obstacles, Dad led the charge, overseeing every detail from fundraising to construction. He did it because he knew the value of a spiritual home—a place where families could gather for generations to come. Today, that synagogue is a vibrant center of community life, a testament to his resolve and his belief in doing what was right, even when it wasn't easy.

My father passed away five years ago, in 2019, from Parkinson's disease, but his legacy shines on in the values he instilled in us. He taught me that true strength lies in humility and grace, and that perseverance can overcome even the greatest challenges. For his wisdom, love, and unwavering belief in me, I will be forever grateful.

Deborah: Sister Power

Deborah is my younger sister—just 22 months behind me—and from the day she arrived, she challenged my status as the center of our parents' universe. Our childhood saw its fair share of sibling rivalry—jockeying for attention, squabbling over toys, and occasionally ganging up on our younger brother. Yet beneath all that, there were also moments of solidarity that hinted we'd be stronger together than we were apart.

Over time, those hints became reality. Life forced Deborah to grow up quickly: by age 23, she was a single mother who had left school to support herself and her child. She started in the only position she could get without a college degree—an administrative assistant. While others might have lamented stalled dreams, Deborah poured her energy into learning everything she could, approaching each task with relentless dedication. Her motto became, "If I'm doing this job, I'm doing it better than anyone expects." That ethic caught the eye of her managers, leading to promotion after promotion—first at UBS, then eventually at IBM.

Her rise to the executive ranks was no small feat. At IBM, she took on the role of Global Sales Leader of Business Analytics, proving that disciplined self-learning and unwavering commitment can triumph over even the toughest odds. Deborah worked harder than anyone else in the room, methodically mastering new skills while also juggling the responsibilities of motherhood. She remained calm under pressure, earned the trust of senior leaders, and turned her office into a place where colleagues sought guidance, knowing she'd give 110% to any challenge.

Meanwhile, I ventured down an entrepreneurial path, marveling at how different our careers looked yet how similar our determination felt. We left behind our childhood competition and discovered an unbreakable bond in adulthood. We call it "sister power"—the magic that happens when two distinct skill sets merge toward a common goal. Our synergy was never more evident than when we came together to care for our parents, navigating the excruciating path of saying goodbye far too soon. In those hardest moments, I realized how grateful I am to have Deborah by my side. Her story reminds me that when sisters unite—combining fierce determination with unwavering support—they become an unstoppable force.

Don Scales: Mentor, Co-Author, Friend

Don Scales came into my life as a client. As the Global CEO who was working on rebranding the company he led, he hired me to design a new logo and what he got was much more. We purposefully redeveloped the company brand. What began as a professional relationship quickly evolved into something far more meaningful. Don was struck by the clarity of my approach to leadership, one that prioritized purpose alongside profit, and he invited me to co-author a book about it.

That book, *How to Lead a Professional Services Firm: The 3 Keys to Drive Purpose and Profit*, was a career-defining moment for me. The experience was transformative, from the writing process to the launch events in London and New York. It felt like the beginning of something extraordinary, a new chapter filled with possibility.

But just as we were on the cusp of expanding and proving our work, Don unexpectedly passed. Losing him was devastating—a harsh reminder of life's fragility. Yet his belief in me and the lessons he taught me continue to inspire me in everything I do. Don wasn't just a mentor; he was a friend who changed my professional trajectory.

Yeeshai Gross: My Partner in Life

A woman once told me, "You're lucky to find love once, let alone twice. Most people don't even find love once." Her words echoed in my mind when I first met Yeeshai, reminding me that sometimes the treasure we seek is right before our eyes—we just need the courage to recognize it.

When people ask how we met, I often joke, "I never dated any of my clients, but I married one." Yet beneath the humor lies a deeper truth: from the start, Yeeshai brought a sense of balance and possibility into my life that I never saw coming. A true collaborator in every sense, he's partnered with many through his creative work—filmmaking, storytelling, and more —and that same spirit of collaboration forms the core of our marriage. He doesn't merely share the load; he amplifies my strengths and pushes me beyond my comfort zone to constantly grow.

At home, Yeeshai is the steady presence in life's storms, the laughter in our chaos, and the calm that keeps our family grounded. He loves with intention, guiding our family with kindness and wisdom that inspires me daily. Watching him build imaginative worlds on screen while nurturing our own world at home reminds me just how fortunate I truly am to share this life with him.

Through Yeeshai, I've learned that love isn't just about "finding" the right person—it's about recognizing them when they appear. Our partnership isn't about completing each other in a clichéd sense but about creating wholeness: two individuals who bring out the best in one another. For all the ways he encourages me, stands beside me, and shows me what true partnership looks like, I am forever grateful.

Gratitude as a Way of Being

Life is filled with moments that challenge, inspire, and shape us. Some arrive as blessings, while others come disguised as

THE HEART OF GRATITUDE: LESSONS IN LOVE, LOSS, AND GROWTH

hardships. But in the end, it's the connections we build, the lessons we learn, and the love we give and receive that matter most.

Gratitude isn't just about looking back with appreciation—it's about living in the present with intention. It's about honoring the people who have shaped us, even in their absence, and recognizing the beauty in life's imperfections.

The hands that shaped me—my family, mentors, friends, and even those who challenged me—are reminders that we are never truly alone on this journey. For that, I am endlessly grateful.

About the Author

Fran Biderman-Gross is an expert in building strong brands, creating effective marketing strategies, and guiding clients through a valuable journey of culture discovery. Since its inception, Fran has used her 3 Keys Technique to contribute to the enduring success of hundreds of companies.

Fran is passionate about helping people stand out so that their full potential can shine. She is also the co-author of the well-received book "How to Lead a Values-Based Professional Services Firm: 3 Keys to Unlock Purpose and Profit" [Wiley 2020].

Connect with Fran:

Email: fran@advantages.net

LinkedIn: www.linkedin.com/in/franbidermangross/

Facebook: facebook.com/FranBGross

Instagram: @franbidermangross

Website: www.advantages.net/

Book: "How to Lead a Values-Based Professional Services Firm: 3 Keys to Unlock Purpose and Profit" – Get your copy at https://3keysbook.com/ or on Amazon.

Podcast: "How to Drive Profit with Purpose" – Listen now at www.3keysbook.com/podcast

CHAPTER 3

Gratitude for My Mother

"When you feel your worst, look your best."
– Laura Kahle

By Dr. Kristin L Kahle

AS I SIT ON A PLANE heading back to Florida to see my parents, I am watching the Martha Stewart Movie and thinking about all the times that my mom brought in items from the Martha Stewart Living Magazine into our childhood. My mom would buy those magazines and create a beautiful home and delicious meals. I wanted to be Martha Stewart so I could create beautiful meals, all while I was young and not at all skilled in the kitchen (absolutely still not good in the kitchen). My mom would shop at Kmart when the Martha Stewart collection came out, and I would go with her to pick up the most beautiful items for our house (not knowing then if we could afford them or not). In so many ways, my mom was a role model to me, just like Martha was to her.

My mother was born in Willard, Ohio, and was raised by her grandmother in that same town. My mom grew up next to her cousins, who were more like brothers for her, and I think they were like her saviors as well. Being raised by her grandmother during that time, there was a stigma around my mother and some bullying that happened throughout her life. My mom had the strength to decide her own course of action for her life and applied for and received a full-ride scholarship to a boarding school for her senior year of high school. While there, she planned to go to college at Duke (also a full ride) but fell so deathly ill that the doctors did not know if she would live or not, so she had to go back to Ohio, find work and start a career.

My mom would say that the best thing about moving back home was meeting my dad a few years later, while he was still in college. Being young and in love, they married right after my dad graduated from college and started their lives together. I am sure that having three children while my father was starting his career as a teacher and a coach in small-town Ohio, with only one car, made it difficult for them to make ends meet. With a very young marriage and young family, my parents were devastated by the news of my brother's childhood cancer. It tore our family apart, emotionally and physically, moving all of us to different locations for a year, having to rely on family and friends to survive this challenging time. My mom decided that it was her fight to fight to save the life of her son, give him the desire to live and get to the other side of cancer. *"Every day is a new chance to begin again"* is a motto that my mom followed every day of her life and one that she wrote for her children in a quote book that she created yearly for us. This quote has been a consistent theme throughout her life.

From childhood to adulthood, my mother has been my guiding light and my inspiration. Talking to my mom daily has always helped to shape my days. At the end of every call, she would say, "Go Get Em." This always allowed me to seize the day and make it great, or at least get through the day knowing that I had my mom to talk with the next day to help with any challenges I was struggling through – from work or school or relationships. I suppose I never knew how lucky I was to have a relationship with my mother that was full of wonderful experiences together. She has been my travel partner, my mentor, and my best friend for my entire life. Even during those horrible teenage years, when no one likes their parents, my mom still inspired me to find the best version of myself and to start creating the life that I wanted to have—that she wanted me to have—including encouraging me to go far away to college knowing that I would thrive, even though she would be so sad every day I wasn't near.

The topic of my chapter centers around my gratitude for my mom and how she has impacted my life. When you start talking about mother-daughter relationships, there are lots of dynamics that define these relationships. Many therapists have made a lot of money around solving or defining these relationships, and there are literally thousands of books on this topic. Think about your relationship with your own mom. What would you change? What words would you use to describe your relationship with your mom? What impact has she had on your life?

On the 22nd of February 2022 (2/22/22—I will always remember), we received the most devastating news that my mother had been diagnosed with Alzheimer's as well as many side effects from this horrible disease. I had been transitioning into a parent for my parents during this time, and not having children of my own, I really struggled with the change. I still wish I could just hear her voice—it is gone now—but I have memories of her words that echo in my head, words of inspiration, and words of pure amusement. Quotes from several books that she loved as well. I crave to hear her laugh now that that is gone as well, so I try every day to get her to smile knowing that she might not know who I am or have any memories of us anymore—I have to carry those memories strong enough and bold enough for the two of us now. I long to have her wisdom when I make life decisions and would love to hear her side of the problem or equation. I desperately want to travel with her and make more memories of a lifetime, memories that I hold onto because they are so dear and precious to my life. And finally, I am lost without my best friend, whom I have been missing since 2022—knowing that I have been so lucky to have my mother as my best friend throughout my life.

My mom always loved reading and collecting poems and quotes throughout her life. In 2005, she created a book of quotes for my brothers and me. It's called *Words of Impact to Me*. When my mom turned 50 on the 16th of August 1995, I compiled the words of wisdom that she said to me throughout my life into a book and gave it to her. I am grateful for these fifty little lessons from my mom. She would share these quotes and use them all to inspire and motivate us to be better children and adults. Some of

GRATITUDE FOR MY MOTHER

these are just plain funny, and I think of them every day. Others have lots of weight to them, and I have used them to shape and model my life.

1. Cover your Ying Yang (there are many words for this, Vijay jay, Who Ha, and others…I am sure each one of you has words for this body part.)

2. First tub at the… First parking spot in the lot

3. Blame your parents when you don't want to do something…My parents won't let me do that—they always wanted to take the blame.

4. When you feel your worst, look your best—I have shared this one in my book, "NOtivation"

5. Learn how to say "I'm so glad to be here" with a smile…My mom said this in a lot of situations when there was nothing else to say.

6. Fill your briefcase with fake stuff. When my mom was going to an interview, I asked her what was in her briefcase, "Fake stuff?" To which she replied, "Yes!"

7. Never, never, never pay full price

8. Wear nylons that match your outfit

9. Never have anything on your countertops

10. Always eat breakfast

11. 28 days, and it's a habit

12. Wait until it goes on sale

13. Park by a light

14. Never walk alone at night

15. Don't start shaving or plucking—always wax

16. It's better to give than receive

17. Never turn down a trip to Ahee's

18. Never eat cheese

19. Body Wise

20. Never know your natural hair color

21. Always serve guests first

GRATITUDE FOR MY MOTHER

22. Never leave without thanking your host/hostess

23. Did you send your "Thank you" notes yet?

24. Less is more

25. Always match your shoes to your purse

26. Power bars…yum or yuck?

27. Look people in the eye

28. Read a book

29. Pack everything in one suitcase

30. Make sure you bring face cream to put on after the flight

31. Feed the missionaries

32. You can't decorate a room without a Longaberger basket

33. Always carry a Thomas Jefferson with you

34. Never send a card without an Andrew Jackson

35. Too many fish in the sea

36. Never drink your calories

37. Once a day, do something unexpected

38. Nothing good ever happens after midnight

39. Compromise is good

40. Don't bite your nails

41. Don't pick at your zits

42. Black hole—does it exist?

43. Hi Ya, Baby!

44. That's my story, and I'm sticking to it

45. Make sure to always have a heart on

46. Go get them…Who are they?

47. Make sure to hide your cords

48. Daddy, Daddy, we want something sweet – sending my Dad to go get us ice cream

49. I love you better than the roast

50. I love you, baby

GRATITUDE FOR MY MOTHER

At my mom's fiftieth birthday party, I read out all the above lessons and quotes that I grew up with and told her how they shaped my life. Closing the book, I gave her the most heartfelt message that I have ever given to her. Besides all of the life lessons and quotes, I told her that she had been an inspiration to me. I said that every time I was with her, I learned something new to take with me to apply to my life. I felt very privileged to have her as my mom and to have her knowledge and guidance in my life. I counted on her to be there in so many ways, and when things came together, they were more beautiful because my mom cared and made an extra effort for my brothers and me. Not only am I fortunate to have her as my mother, but anyone that comes into contact with her is lucky to know her as well. With her power, she has touched so many lives. With all that knowledge and love, anyone that has come into contact with my mom has been lucky. "But you see, my dear mother," I said to her, "I am the luckiest of all because I have had you as my best friend, my mentor, my guide, my strength, my hope, my peace, my knowledge, and the very best mother I could ever want."

I have so many memories of my mother that are very precious to me and have shaped my life. Not only all the quotes above but also all the memories and fun that we have had together. While I am watching my mother in the long goodbye chapter of her life, I am grateful for the strength she has given me. I am sure that I would not be the same woman I am without her. What I will take with me in this next phase of life with my mom is gratitude. Gratitude for the lessons that have shaped my life and for having those lessons to share with my friends and family so that my mom's legacy continues long after she is gone. Gratitude for the relationship that I have had with her and the privilege of having it, as many others crave to have that same relationship with their mothers. And finally, gratitude for the knowledge of my first real teacher in life. This is not goodbye to my mother, but certainly a homage to her and the impact that she has made on my life and the lives of all of the others that she has touched as well.

About the Author

Dr. Kristin Kahle is a trailblazing business leader who broke through barriers in a male-dominated industry. By the age of 30, she made her first million, sold a company, and founded NavigateHCR (NHCR), a successful HR and compliance technology firm. Juggling personal and professional challenges, Kristin has shown that it's possible to thrive in business while supporting other women.

Her unconventional path began with her fascination with insurance, inspired by her father's work. She pursued a business degree, excelling in accounting and statistics after overcoming academic struggles in high school. Kristin's background as an athlete helped her develop time management and resilience, skills that she carried into her career.

Today, as the founder of NHCR, she leads a multi-million-dollar enterprise and mentors young entrepreneurs, especially women. A recognized expert in healthcare reform, Kristin continues to create innovative solutions and inspire future generations of female leaders.

Connect with Kristin:

Email: hello@drkristinkahle.com

Website: drkristinkahle.com

CHAPTER 4

The Golden Glue: An Essay on Gratitude

"You may not control all the events that happen to you, but you can decide not to be reduced by them."

– Maya Angelou

By Effie Bar-Caspi

GRATITUDE HAS A WAY OF GROUNDING US, connecting us to others and to parts of ourselves we might have otherwise lost along the way. When I think about gratitude in my life, it is less about isolated moments and more about a mosaic—pieces from my past, each one representing a person or memory that held me up, mended a crack, or showed me how to love. They are the moments and people who shaped me into who I am today, giving me a foundation on which to build my own life and family. Each of these memories is like a broken piece, a part of me that holds both joy and pain, and they are precious fragments that make up my story. In the art of "kintsugi"—the Japanese tradition of mending broken pottery with gold—the cracks are filled with golden lacquer, creating a piece that is even more beautiful for its history and flaws. In my life, my memories are the broken pieces, some filled with pain and sorrow, some filled with love, guidance, and resilience. Each person I met became a part of my art, another broken piece of my heart. Yet it is my husband who is the golden glue, holding all those pieces together and creating a wholeness that has helped me heal from the inside out.

The journey to gratitude began with an unexpected experience during a facilitation training session, where a moment of reflection opened a doorway to healing and appreciation that I had not realized I needed.

Revisiting Broken Pieces

I remember sitting in that training session, my heart heavy as the facilitator instructed us to think back to sixth grade, a time when we may have struggled academically or personally. She asked us to recall a subject that challenged us and to imagine ourselves at that age—twelve years old—perhaps facing our first real difficulties. As her words washed over us, she encouraged us to remember if there had been an adult in our life who helped us during those struggles. I immediately thought of my English lessons at that age, a time when I felt utterly alone. My parents, though loving, weren't able to help me directly with school assignments. They were facing struggles of their own, challenges that affected the emotional environment of our home. I knew they weren't available to support me emotionally at that time, and while they did what they could—like arranging for private tutoring—the underlying emotional neglect left an ache in my life. I felt a quiet sadness, a kind of loneliness I couldn't yet name, as I realized I couldn't lean on them in the way I needed. The teacher who tutored me, who was meant to support me, was just another adult who let me down; rather than helping, she amplified my sense of inadequacy and isolation, leaving me feeling even more defeated.

As I stood there in the training room, I could feel a familiar ache in my chest: "I'm a failure, I'm not good enough…" And then, the facilitator spoke words that pierced through my memories. She said, "And if you didn't have an adult at that point in your life who was there for you, I am so sorry." Hearing that line, I felt an unexpected flood of emotion, a kind of sadness that I had been carrying unknowingly, layered with a longing for support I hadn't known how to ask for. But this moment was also a turning point. As I processed those words in the days that followed, I found myself looking at my past differently. I realized that, while I didn't have that support as a twelve-year-old, I had been blessed with a series of profound relationships and experiences that, over time, helped me gather the pieces and heal. I could now see the strength, wisdom, and encouragement I'd found in others who became the mentors and companions I'd once lacked. Each person I met became a part of my art, a piece of my broken heart, slowly mending me over the years and shaping my future.

My Grandmother:
The Embrace of Unconditional Love

The first piece of my gratitude story begins with my grandmother, whose hugs I can still feel to this day. Her hugs were pure, unburdened by expectation, long and warm, and enveloped me in a love that asked nothing in return. She would call me her "Neshume," her soul in Yiddish, and that's exactly how I felt—like I was part of her spirit, cherished and embraced. Her love was simple and true, the kind of love that asks nothing, that is given simply because it is there to give. In a life where I often felt pressure to please or be a "good girl," her love was a sanctuary, a reminder that I was enough as I was. I didn't need to earn it, nor could I lose it.

I have since come to realize how rare that kind of love is, and how much I needed it. My grandmother's love taught me that we all need a place where we can simply be, where love is given freely, a place of rest and acceptance. That is the kind of love I am grateful to give to my own children now. I want them to know they are seen and cherished just as they are, just as my grandmother saw me. In my life today, I carry her love forward, holding my children close with the same warmth and gentleness that she gave to me.

My Aunt: A Legacy of Family and Tradition

My aunt, like my grandmother, has deeply influenced my vision for both my marriage and the legacy I hope to build. She holds an essential place in my heart and has shown me the kind of relationship I aspire to have with my husband. As a child, we would gather with her family at my grandparents' house, celebrating holidays and birthdays together. Those gatherings were filled with laughter, food, and togetherness, creating memories that became a source of comfort and happiness. As I grew older, I would visit Israel with my own children to her home to reunite with my cousins and their children. There, we continued to create new memories. Through all these years, my aunt has held us together, carrying forward the legacy my grandmother had built.

Her home is filled with love, warmth, and the deep-rooted traditions of our family. Despite the devastating loss of her own child—my cousin—she has continued to keep the family close, nurturing the bonds between us and creating a space where love persists. Her strength and resilience inspire me; even in the face of pain, she keeps family traditions alive, celebrating life with those of us who remain. She has taught me that love and family can endure, that a family's heart beats on in every gathering, and that we can carry forward our heritage through each generation. I am grateful for her dedication to our family, which has inspired me to build the same foundation for my own family.

The Family I Worked With: Lessons of Strength and Resilience

Another piece of my gratitude journey comes from a family I worked with while I was in law school. I had taken a job helping care for their youngest daughter, who was disabled, and over time, I became part of their lives as they became part of mine forever. I spent countless hours over four years with them, and in those hours, I learned about the kind of love, communication skills, and patience needed to keep a family strong. Despite the challenges that came with caring for their daughter, the parents' relationship stood as a model of trust, respect, and unwavering commitment. They faced each difficulty together, finding ways to support one another through both joy and struggle.

In their home, I saw how resilience was woven into everyday life, where all their children thrived, supported by the warmth and stability of their family. Watching the love and respect in their marriage, I realized this was the kind of partnership I wanted for myself—a relationship built on mutual respect, trust, and a shared commitment to our family. This family showed me that no matter the struggles we face, love, resilience, and unity can help us weather any storm. I am forever grateful for the time I spent with them, for they gave me a vision of the relationship and values I wanted to build in my own life.

My Husband: The Golden Lacquer That Holds Everything Together

The last and most vital part of my gratitude story is my husband—not just a single piece of my life but the golden lacquer that holds every piece together, binding my joys, struggles, and memories into something whole and beautiful. My golden glue. He is my partner, my support, and my "kintsugi," the person who brings together all the pieces that have made me who I am, creating a mosaic that shines through each scar, each success, each memory.

We met when I was nineteen, and over the past twenty-five years, he has been the one who has believed in me fully, even in the moments when I doubted myself. His unwavering faith in me has helped bridge every divide within my heart. He hasn't just been one of the good influences in my life; he is the golden thread that holds all of my experiences—both the good and the difficult—in unity, transforming each memory into part of a beautiful, complete picture. He sees me fully, embracing each broken piece and creating something whole, something greater than the sum of its parts.

Several years ago, at a couple's event, we did an exercise envisioning our life goals. I wrote down my dream of a family home, like my aunt's, that would become a center for future generations—a place where our children, and eventually our grandchildren, could gather to celebrate and create memories together. Not long after, we found the perfect home, a place large enough for my dream, though beyond what we could afford. My husband's steadfast support and belief in that vision gave me the courage to pursue it. He assured me that our children should grow up with these memories now, not just someday in the future. Together, we made it happen. His trust in me, in my values, encouraged me not to give up on my dreams.

Today, we are raising our family in that home, filled with love, laughter, and the traditions of our heritage. Each celebration, each moment, carries forward the legacy of love and unity I strive to provide for our children, giving them a healthier foundation, a sense of safety, and unconditional love. Doron, my husband, as his name means, is a gift in my life. With his support and ability to see me as I am, to love me as I am, he holds all of the pieces of

THE GOLDEN GLUE: AN ESSAY ON GRATITUDE

my heart with his golden, shining lacquer, supporting me to be better, to be whole, to be complete. As I am.

Reflecting on that moment in the training session, when the facilitator asked if we had someone who had been there for us in a time of need—and then said, "I'm so sorry if you didn't have one"—I felt the weight of the past and the loneliness of those early years. But over time, I've come to understand that finding a partner like my husband has changed everything. With his unwavering love, belief, and support, he has woven together my past, present, and future, transforming even the painful memories into something whole and beautiful. His presence is the gold that has filled every crack, embracing every experience, both good and bad, and creating a life where I am truly seen, encouraged, and loved. He holds my mosaic of memories together, mending and reflecting on all that has been and all that is yet to come.

About the Author

Effie Bar-Caspi is a distinguished entrepreneur, leadership facilitator, and founder of CorePoration Inc., whose diverse career spans military service, law, and financial services. Her professional journey began with service in the Israel Defense Forces, followed by establishing an independent law practice after earning her LLB degree. Drawing from her experience, Bar-Caspi co-founded a successful tax and accounting firm in Seattle, Washington.

THE GOLDEN GLUE: AN ESSAY ON GRATITUDE

Over twelve years of entrepreneurship, Bar-Caspi demonstrated exceptional skill in building corporate infrastructure and optimizing organizational systems, consistently driving growth while maximizing return on investment. Throughout her career, she has earned recognition for her outstanding leadership abilities and communication skills, consistently demonstrating a talent for building trust with both internal teams and external stakeholders, and fostering workplace cultures that promote high morale, engagement, and employee retention.

Now as a Leadership Facilitator, Bar-Caspi helps others develop authentic leadership styles founded on trust, while dividing her time between global travel, mentoring fellow entrepreneurs, and active community service. Based in the Pacific Northwest, she lives with her husband of over twenty years and their four children, exemplifying her commitment to balancing professional excellence with family life and community engagement.

CHAPTER 5

Gratitude And...

*"When you can't find someone to follow,
you have to find a way to lead by example."*
—Roxane Gay, "Bad Feminist"

By Shenandoah Davis

I VIVIDLY REMEMBER THE FIRST TIME I witnessed someone get fired. I was working at an Asian fusion restaurant in the Pike Place Market in Seattle as a server/bartender. We were coming off of a particularly challenging shift – we had a huge group in for private dining, a bunch of drunk cruise ship passengers demanding cocktails we had never heard of, and a couple of co-workers who were out sick. We were in the weeds for hours, barely getting to wipe tables down and find a place to move stacks of dirty dishes before new, eager, and impatient customers sat down. When things died down, and we were trying to reclaim a semblance of normal, one of the longest-running servers had a full meltdown and ended up screaming at the restaurant owner. "YOU NEVER SAY THANK YOU!" she said, crying hysterically while all of us sort of awkwardly watched while we pretended to wipe down countertops a safe distance away. "I WORKED SO HARD FOR YOU TONIGHT, AND YOU DIDN'T EVEN SAY THANK YOU!" The owner, without batting an eye, looked at her calmly and simply said, "I say thank you with money. Please go home."

She left, and the rest of us continued cleaning up, a little wide-eyed from the experience. As a twenty-something, I wasn't really sure who was right or wrong in the scenario – only that expectations had been reset for our roles at the company. We came to work, we left, we got paid. That was the job, and for most of us as aspiring artists, musicians, or students, that was plenty.

Every working relationship possesses some form of this dichotomy, although it's rarely quite so black and white. Work is where we spend most of our lives, and company culture has shifted to "work families" and "work wives." Companies are encouraged to holistically support every aspect of their employees' lives, with differing opinions on the spectrum of conscious capitalism of where and how to fit professional boundaries within a world of hypothetical work-life balance that seems to mean we're usually too tired by thinking about all the work we need to do that we barely have the energy to do any of the work.

These days, I run a private recruitment firm that helps hundreds of families live meaningful lives on their own terms by introducing them to dynamic, world-traveling nannies, private educators, and newborn care specialists. As I write this, our company is completing the final steps of submitting for B Corp certification, and our team of 18 has never been stronger, smarter, and more connected. I live in what can only be described as my "dream home" in western North Carolina: a funky brick house built in the 1950s by the heir to a department store magnate. While I occasionally find myself working late nights or weekends to respond to emails, overall, I feel satisfied, proud, and grateful for the organization I've built, for my family, my team, and for the many nannies and families we've supported. However, my relationship with gratitude has *significantly* evolved over the past two decades.

GRATITUDE AND...

Gratitude has always been a complex word for me. It is challenging to separate gratitude from the idea of being deserving or being worthy. What I am now coming to understand is that both things can be true: you can receive gifts, rewards, and accolades that you deserve, and you can feel and express deep and profound gratitude for them that has nothing to do with external rewards.

Slowly growing a team of three people to nearly twenty at Adventure Nannies over the past nine years has felt like an exercise in setting and resetting expectations; of thinking that you've given generously from a place of gratitude, only to realize later there were unspoken expectations and assumptions attached to your generosity that even you were unaware of; of oscillating between feeling taken advantage of and feeling guilty for never quite offering enough.

There are stages of gratitude when you're growing a business. Here are a few of the stages I've oscillated between for days or even years.

Non-Deserving Gratitude. The first person who works for you will be an angel who descended from the heavens and will save your life, your marriage, your business, and your sanity. They can do no wrong because they have given you back freedom and your own time. Any mistakes they make are likely your fault since you're the one who trained them, right?! You're just grateful they show up every day, and you're terrified of them leaving.

Gaslit Gratitude. Directed towards the employee who never skips a beat on making sure you know exactly how amazing they are, how many other opportunities are available to them, and how fortunate you are that, for today, they chose you – but you better not screw it up.

MLM-Energy Gratitude. This is the type of gratitude that erupts like a volcano of toxic positivity during all-hands meetings, with the intent to inspire everyone around you, but somehow leaves you sad and empty because, somehow, none of it ever ricochets back to you.

Conditional Gratitude. To some, it may register as future thinking, to some as manifesting, but it's the act of gratitude that leaves you expressing gratitude for things that haven't quite come to fruition yet – leaving behind the things you have going for you at this moment.

GRATITUDE AND...

While I've always been a proponent of gratitude and seen others experience the benefits of living a life full of gratitude, I can't say I really "got it" until this past year. Not for lack of trying—I've made the lists, done the journals, covered my desk with Post-Its reminding myself to thank people and make sure they felt appreciated. (This project quickly fell apart when I neglected to throw away the Post-Its after thanking people and ended up thanking my employees multiple times for completing the same task, which just gave them the creeps.) I couldn't shift my own mindset from feeling grateful to just *being* grateful or shake the idea that feeling or expressing too much gratitude meant somehow that I didn't deserve whatever kindness had been shown to *me*. I couldn't really quantify or justify the balance between receiving something you've earned—like an award, a promotion, success in business—and still being grateful for it. Working hard and striving for accolades has always been extremely important and motivating to me, and somehow, feeling gratitude for that almost felt like a way of belittling my own accomplishments or taking credit *away* from myself.

2024 was the hardest year I've experienced as a business owner, but also the one that has left me with a new, profound understanding of gratitude and an overwhelming cup filled with gratitude for my business and my team. When a key employee who had been with me nearly since inception left the team to help grow a family business, I stepped back into the trenches with grand plans on how I, the fearless force of nature behind the brand, could steer our client team (our primary source of revenue) ready to make sweeping changes and sprinkle a healthy dusting of CEO magic all over the company. Instead, seven weeks into the year, my youngest sibling (they/them) was diagnosed with breast cancer. They didn't have insurance or a job at the time, so a flurry of sorting through Medicare applications, disability forms, doctor's appointments, scheduling, and remotely communicating with our extended family and their amazing partner quickly took over as my main/only priority. I resigned from boards, dropped out of accountability groups and meetings, shut down my consultancy, and for a few months, operated on an "if you need me, call me" schedule at my business.

I did so with the full knowledge that, if I had been an employee at most businesses, right around two weeks of this is likely when I would have lost my job. In fact, I'm ashamed to say that a few months earlier in the business, we'd had a "heart-to-heart" with a newer employee who had missed a considerable amount of work due to several family emergencies of their own that had all happened concurrently. Reeling from losing someone who had been a true anchor of our business for so many years, I braced myself for an inevitable exodus of employees and could imagine the very valid reasons they would have for jumping ship—or, worse—phoning it in at their jobs, knowing I wasn't able to pay much attention or give much more than the bare minimum.

Instead, something miraculous happened that has re-wired my brain and my outlook on gratitude: for the most part, the team stayed. They stepped up and took on new responsibilities. An assistant I had barely trained suddenly took over my inbox and calendar and held the fort down when I was unexpectedly traveling or tied up on hold with various government agencies trying to sort out care. A new leader I had built out a six-month training and transition plan for took over 90% of the role two weeks later without anything more to work from than a one-page document about my thoughts on her new role I had jotted down. Employees who had never spoken in public before said yes to flying across the country to deliver presentations to groups of nannies in unfamiliar settings and cities.

Within all of this, the numbers started to reflect this new sense of teamwork that I never could have taught or trained—our revenue went up by nearly 20%, and our profit went up by over 30%. My leadership team gracefully accepted my time and energy when I was able to offer it and steered the ship when I didn't – without a second thought.

Did this happen because I, as a leader, created an environment of generosity, safety, and gratitude? Did it happen because I just have the most amazing team of humans committed to my company? Did it happen because everyone felt sorry for me? Was it just an oversight? Was my team happy to get me temporarily out of the way and finally run things as they saw fit? While I'm problematically prone to anxiety and over-analyzing any and every scenario, this time, I just didn't. I was just grateful. It didn't come down to merit or what anyone owed me—I remembered my restaurant days—they were getting paid. Despite whatever company culture I had strived to create, however many group trips or retreats I had organized, whatever acts of kindness I had struggled to give to my team, and the overwhelm of being concerned as to whether or not they were appreciated, I knew that at the end of the day, that restaurant owner's words rang true in any job. People show up to make money.

On Monday, my sibling completed their last radiation treatment, and we've been told that the odds of a breast cancer re-occurrence is less than 0.1%. I've stepped back into the day-to-day of my business and have been warmly welcomed back by my team, although everyone agreed that most of the responsibilities they took on unexpectedly at the beginning of the year made sense on their plates, so my role has shifted to kind of a dream role that many entrepreneurs map out but never get to achieve. I get to live in the clouds and only occasionally visit the weeds. I get to speak at conferences and pursue my own personal development, which has led to having the time and energy to map out professional and personal development pathways for everyone on our team. I got to run a full-scale retreat called Nanny Camp, where over seventy nannies came from across the country to sleep in cabins, make s'mores, sing around campfires, and forge new friendships in an industry that can be incredibly isolating. I even launched a book club within our company, which means I now get to pay my employees to read and bring new ideas to their teams!

In a true moment of crisis for myself and my family, the team I built at my company stepped up in incredible ways without being asked and *without* expecting anything in return. Anyone who has been through a life-altering event, a long-term health issue, or a family emergency knows that in these moments, the folks who continue to show up for you, check in on you, support you, and celebrate you are rarely the ones who you expected to be there. In the year my family needed me, *my employees* were there for me in ways I will never forget—and I will never think about building, growing, or retaining talent in the same way ever again. Not only did I get to go back and forth from North Carolina to Philadelphia and be there for surgeries and follow-ups, splitting up caretaking shifts with my parents and other siblings, but I also took time off to create unforgettable memories with my family. I took my sibling to Las Vegas in between their rounds of chemo to see Lady Gaga perform a jazz set with a big-band orchestra, and I celebrated my father's retirement on the Oregon coast. We all came together, and in many ways, our family is now closer than ever. My time away from the office was never questioned by my leadership team—they had the grace to assume and understand that any time I was spending time and energy elsewhere was, as we often say at Adventure Nannies, that I was "doing the needful."

Our team at Adventure Nannies has become a chosen family, and while people come and go and do all of the unpredictable things that humans do, my mission as a CEO and business owner has evolved to make sure the organization I'm building has both the capacity and the heart to support each other *fully* and prepare for the moments that any of us need support and a strong foundation to depend on.

While it took a life-altering event for me to reset and evolve my relationship with gratitude, getting out of my comfort zone and separating gratitude from questions of worthiness has lightened my psyche in every way. Getting to experience grace, compassion, and patience on a human level from my employees in my biggest moment of need has inspired me to find new ways to extend kindness to those around me. The opportunity to come to work *every day* with genuine gratitude for the work I get to do and the team I get to do it with has renewed my passion for my business and given me new goals to strive for. I *can* feel grateful for anything—including things I accomplished—without that same anxiety of worthiness accompanying it. I can feel lucky for the experiences and memories I've gotten to form *and* feel that I've **earned** them simultaneously. I can give more freely of my time, energy, and resources to others without thinking of it as an exchange or quid pro quo. I no longer sit over my morning coffee, tapping my pen on my desk, struggling to write down five things I am grateful for each morning. I am alive. My sibling is alive. I have a partner and animals that can't wait for me to finish working every day. I have a team that has truly become friends and chosen family, whom I know I can rely on in the moments I need them most—and who can rely on me. I can be grateful *and* want more. I can be grateful *and* kind to myself. And from now on, I will be.

About the Author

Shenandoah Davis is a CEO, co-founder, and consultant who embraces projects that support women in the workforce. Her recruitment firm, Adventure Nannies, has won excellence and innovation awards in their industry and is currently working towards their BHAG of sending the first nanny to space. She is the founder of Invisible Consulting, a full-scale consultancy firm assisting business owners in the recruitment, staffing, and birthing industries to grow and scale their businesses. Shenandoah has been profiled in Forbes Women, both for her work at Adventure Nannies and with Nanny Relief Fund, the only 501(c)3 dedicated to providing need-based grants to nannies experiencing hardship. In her free time, she loves traveling, learning new languages, and entertaining family and friends. She lives outside of Asheville, North Carolina, with her husband and dogs. This is her second contribution to the *Lead Like A Woman* anthology series.

Connect with Shenandoah:

shenandoah@adventurenannies.com

https://www.linkedin.com/in/shenandoah-davis-a1b818b/

CHAPTER 6

Finding Grace

There is nothing enlightened about shrinking so that other people won't feel insecure around you. And as we let our own light shine, we unconsciously give other people permission to do the same."
—Marianne Williamson

By Adrienne Palmer

I HAVE CREATED MULTIPLE SUCCESSFUL businesses and had three business exits, providing me the financial independence to live life on my own terms. I have a supportive, loving marriage based on true partnership, authenticity, and personal growth. My husband and I are living full-time aboard our sailing yacht, traveling the world, currently based in the Mediterranean. It sounds like a dream.

To fully understand the depth of my gratitude for this life, you would have had to know me as a teenager. The probability of creating a life of fulfillment, success, and adventure was low. Coming from a childhood of poverty, abuse, and neglect, I was in a desperate situation. My broken family was often homeless, sleeping at roadside motels or hiding out at trailer parks in rural Florida. Always in survival mode, fighting to get through life. After 22 school-age relocations, I learned to blend in and stay in the background. Life was about fear, anxiety, secrecy, and pain. It was hard for a little girl. By age 14, with the help of an empathetic, not always rule-following, high school guidance counselor, I started living alone, paying my own household bills, and working full-time. It was better than the alternative.

As easily as I could have found excuses for why my hardships in life were not my fault, I chose a different perspective. I learned a lot of lessons from my childhood. Resilience, work ethic, adaptability, and the importance of community and a support network. From seeing the dark side of humanity and the world, I somehow emerged as an optimist. I am often called a bit of a Pollyanna. Maybe, deep in my soul, I knew there was a brighter future ahead. And for that inner knowing, I am grateful.

Grateful for a Fresh Start

An invitation from a Texas university was my ticket out. That guidance counselor who helped me get a work permit at age 14 also spent his time searching for scholarships for which I might qualify. He knew I had no money, but my academic credentials were strong. He pushed me to present a polished impression. I wrote copious essays, diligently completed applications, and developed a resume showcasing my responsibility, creativity, and willingness to work hard. It worked.

I packed my Toyota hatchback with whatever I could fit inside to start over. I drove through the night and started a new life in Texas. I clearly remember my mantras from that time: *I can start over, leave the past behind. This does not define me. I get to choose my own life path. I am ultimately responsible.*

Self-preservation led me to keep my personal story to myself. I made no mention of my parents or family and always answered questions about my past vaguely. Compartmentalization became a superpower. It was the fresh start I needed, and Florida was literally in the rearview mirror. I am truly grateful to have had that chance to just drive away and begin anew.

My willingness to be vulnerable and transparent came years later, after a lot of personal growth, introspection, and questioning "WHY." I am proud, now, of owning the entirety of myself, including my past, as part of what makes me who and how I am: scars, warts, and all.

Grateful for Good Timing

I continued my seeking of self through a variety of career paths. By my mid-20s, I had covered retail store clerk, music industry promotions, banking, travel agent, horse racing management, and investor relations for public companies, just to name a few. I finally realized the only possible answer for such a wayward soul: I was an entrepreneur. Every new idea seemed fun to pursue, like a new adventure, a new possibility. The good news was that I had the natural ability to see opportunities and to connect and engage others. I also had the grit and work ethic to push harder than most of my peers.

It was the late 1990s when technology was opening up a whole new world of industries to be explored. It was just the fertile ground I needed to put my own stake in the ground. Good timing, indeed!

Motivated by a literal pat on the head from a former boss when expressing my excitement for this new fad called *the internet*, I started my first real business (Insite) in 1998 and haven't worked for anyone else since. In an environment dominated by young men with a geeky bend, I was the 20-something woman who came from a business and marketing perspective and helped clients see the practical advantages of the emerging technology. As the company grew, I hand-selected team members who focused on business use case benefits and understanding the why of the online systems we created. When things got tough, the team I built dug into the commitment to quality work, and we still managed to have a great time doing it. For them, I am grateful.

Insite's great timing led us to proudly declare ourselves first at accomplishing a lot of things, always innovating and always having a shiny new example of what can be done on the internet. We have a trophy case packed full of hundreds of innovation awards to prove it, and that fed my need for acceptance and accolades in the business community.

We navigated some hard times, too: the dot com crash, the 9/11 aftermath, the 2008 economic crisis. It wasn't all fun and games. There were rounds of layoffs, bank negotiations that felt like gunfight standoffs, fraud, theft, and lawsuits. But I persevered, and those lessons from my childhood about self-reliance, work ethic, and adaptability served me well.

The *Dallas Business Journal* wrote an article about me with the headline "*Techno Tenacity.*" I am not sure if they realized at the time how tenacious I had been all my life, but the headline seemed to get attention.

Starting Insite, and running the company for 19 years, gave me insight into my own abilities and who I am as a person and as a leader, my strengths, what energized me, and what depleted me. Knowing these things about myself would serve me well in the future. For me, the fun part was the team leadership, finding talented people willing to work hard, and providing an environment to thrive and grow. We built a culture of mutual support and trust and of taking great pride in the work we created for clients.

Grateful for Community

I am the epitome of fierce independence. I always have been. I am used to going at it alone and surviving. I am used to being the outlier, frequently misunderstood. But entrepreneurship is a lonely journey. Everything was new, different, uncharted. There were so many things I had to figure out on my own. I was not afraid of figuring things out, but I came to realize that I was at a disadvantage for having never been taught anything about running a business. I quickly found myself seeking experience and craving relatability.

In those early days of Insite, on my makeshift desk, made of two stacks of boxes and a wood board in a storage room of another company, I toiled away on my own. I heard through the grapevine of our startup-focused office building about a group of entrepreneurs who would meet and share experiences to help one another. AH HA! This is what I need! Upon learning that I needed to have over $1M in top-line revenue to join, it was just the motivation I needed to make it happen. One client at a time, adding one employee, then another, then another. Imagine my pride when I looked at my P&L and saw the $1M 12-month average clearly in sight! By May 2000, I was a full-fledged member of the Entrepreneurs' Organization (EO).

It was as if a new world had opened up for me. People understood the emotions I was feeling and the challenges I was navigating. I was not alone. I was not as wayward and inadequate as I thought. I learned that other business owners that I thought had it all figured out were just as uncertain as I was. When I felt out of my depth, I could admit it. And even if no one had the answer, they had a genuine shoulder to lean on. It was the tribe, the community I needed. I was grateful. I still am, and always will be, grateful.

My gratitude for this community led me to serve in all levels of leadership, volunteering my time to help other entrepreneurs feel less alone and building a strong community that could help take our members to new heights in their leadership, their access to resources, and their personal growth. After many years of serving my local Dallas chapter, I was asked to serve in international leadership positions and, eventually, on the Global Board of Directors. Working with entrepreneurs worldwide tapped into a new sense of connection and purpose for me and taught me unparalleled lessons in leadership, diplomacy, politics, organizational dynamics, and human behavior.

Grateful for a Clarity of Purpose

Long before my term on the Global Board of Directors of EO, my global citizen heart was starting to take shape. I noticed my own emotional reaction to cross-cultural breakdowns, the protectiveness that would well up. The justice warrior inside of me was ready to take a stand. I often wondered how I could channel that energy to increasing connection and understanding. Until more recently, I could not explain why it resonated so deeply with me, but I knew it was a call that must be answered.

As a first-generation American born to a holocaust survivor, I know the impact of closed-mindedness, judgment, and bigotry. I know firsthand the deep scars that carry forward through generations and the unnecessary suffering it creates. I made the choice many years ago to be a global citizen. A person who wants to engage with the myriad of cultures in our world. A person willing to be uncomfortable, embarrassed, scared, stretched, and challenged. Any chance to build a bridge, and get people to see each other as individuals with the same human needs and dreams as their own, is an empowering moment for me.

I eagerly accepted the invitation to join a non-profit board of business leaders focused on global awareness and cross-cultural relations. The experience opened my mind to the role of business in this endeavor. Businesses that sell products in other countries, to people of other cultures, can either positively or negatively impact diplomatic relationships and human understanding.

When I was connected to the US State Department to collaborate on a project to build trust and understanding among entrepreneurs from around the world, to say I was struck by a calling would be an understatement. It was the intersection of the crossroads of my life. I led the programming of *A New Beginning: Entrepreneurship and Business Innovation* for 4 years, and it changed my life and the lives of the 120 delegates from 80 countries that were a part of it. We proved the power entrepreneurship had to build connections, and the US State Department, to this day, reflects on it as one of the most powerful diplomatic programs to date. As the program came to its close, I began my EO Global Board service and continued to advise on panels and participate in collaborations with the White House, United Nations, and other global entrepreneurship NGOs.

I am grateful for knowing that feeling of clarity of purpose. The feeling in my chest, pulling me forward, knowing with certainty that I was contributing to the world something that was not only making a positive impact but that I had the unique qualifications and passion to execute. I am not sure when or how such clarity of purpose will show up in my life again, but I trust that I will recognize it when it does and be ready to answer the call.

Grateful for Second Chances

After my EO Global Board and global diplomacy experience, I knew that running a tech company in Dallas could no longer hold my soul and fulfill my purpose. I stepped away from the daily running of Insite in 2017 and sold the majority of my shares in the company. That decision was the right one for me at the time, but it left me feeling twinges of regret and disappointment. I knew I needed to move to the next chapter of my life, but I can recognize in hindsight that I did not adequately prepare the team and did not tee up succession in the company to ensure the preservation of the values the company was built on. I accepted a less-than-optimal buyout in exchange for the freedom to follow my heart. At my retirement dinner, I was gifted a clock necklace, which is a constant reminder that the most significant part of the sale was receiving the gift of time for my next pursuit.

About a year and a half later, my life partner, Peter, became my business partner as well. The company he had started 10 years prior, Skvare, was doing well but remained dependent on him for most every task. It was, admittedly, me who resisted the blatantly obvious truth that what was needed was exactly my strengths: team leadership, finding talented people willing to work hard, and providing an environment to thrive and grow. Once Peter and I teamed up and focused on our strengths, we were unstoppable. I brought in the talent and kept them motivated and learning. Peter focused on the technology and quality standards in delivery. I had never experienced having a true business partner before, one I could rely on to carry equal weight and responsibility. Being able to focus on my own lane and only do what energizes and fulfills me was freeing and brought its own rewards.

As much as our sale of Skvare created financial freedom, it also created a fulfillment of the soul. Building a team, with the lessons of succession and leadership learned from Insite, allowed me to fully appreciate and internalize my own abilities.

It was the second chance I needed to convince my inner self-doubting, imposter syndrome voice to quiet down. I am grateful to have had that opportunity.

Grateful for Lessons Learned

I am often asked what leadership lessons I would share with other women navigating challenges in business and in life. While everyone's journey is their own, I can share a few thoughts that resonate most deeply for me.

- Only you can choose your future. Not other people, not life circumstances, not disadvantages you may have at the starting line. Having a clear vision and a committed mindset, combined with a bit of grit and resilience, can overcome a lot of obstacles.

- You don't have to do it alone. As much as we, as women, pride ourselves on independence and self-reliance, there are communities and resources available to make the journey easier and less lonely.

- Our feminine traits, which are often considered weaknesses in business, can also be our superpowers.

Vulnerability creates a human connection and can create relationships of trust and a genuine interest in helping one another. Our sensitive emotions give us our intuitive ability to read people and foresee challenges before they occur.

- Know thyself. Understand your own strengths, passions, weaknesses, and flaws. A willingness to do the inner growth work is an uncommon trait that can pay great dividends when choosing partners, delegating responsibilities, and determining which next paths to pursue.

Grateful for Finding Grace

After 40 years of full-time work and pushing boulders uphill, it was time to exhale. It was enough. I had fought enough, proven enough, overcome enough, accomplished enough, earned enough, and impacted enough. Enough to stop the grasping and desperate seeking of approval. Enough to put down my sword.

Transforming from a fiercely independent, angry, hurt young girl to a woman of self-acceptance and self-love was not an easy metamorphosis. For many decades, I saw struggle as a part of the grander nature of life, not as an adversary. I accepted suffering as normal. Without it… well, I wonder if, at times, I would manifest some just to feel like I was doing it right.

Gratitude has gotten me through so many challenges in life. I've often felt the universe (or God, if you prefer) conspiring in my favor. Setting up opportunities for me to discover the next opening toward a brighter future. Combined with my optimism and hope, gratitude brought me to grace.

Through learning to sail, my husband and I found a different flow—a different way of being. Learning to sail is a journey of self-discovery, pushing through the uncomfortable. It requires fortitude and self-reliance. Sometimes, it requires facing your deepest fears. And, in the moments of finding harmony with nature, there is nothing like the feeling of cutting through the water, sails full, being propelled forward by only the wind. We spent several years living aboard a sailboat part-time, traveling to new places, and feeding our nomadic spirits.

After the last business sale in 2023, we made the decision to make sailing our full-time lifestyle. We sold our home and our cars and gave away almost everything we owned. In a matter of months, I deconstructed the life it took three decades to build in exchange for the opportunity to be truly free to discover what's next. Of course, the treasured friendships and deep sisterly bonds I've gathered along the way come with me, regardless of geography. For those, I am eternally grateful.

And now, I am grateful to have the freedom to be truly present and fully immersed aboard our sailing yacht, S/Y GRACE. Yes, we named our sailboat GRACE. We came to realize that grace is why we are here. We love the grace of sailing. Even more so, we love the grace we continue to learn in handling challenges, in navigating life, and in our relationships with each other and those we meet along our journey. We even find grace in moments when things go terribly wrong, which they sometimes do when sailing. When equipment breaks or nature creates unexpectedly dangerous conditions or we find ourselves under pressure to problem—solve our way out of a precarious situation.

We hope to be vessels of grace in our own hearts and to spread grace as we travel and explore. My self-reflection and introspection will continue. Finding grace is not a one-and-done endeavor. I am not perfect at it, and it is a constant effort to show up as the person I strive to be.

My passion and calling to make a positive impact in the world burns strong, as does my belief that every human being can be a light that shines and inspires others to shine as well. I look forward to discovering new ways to create global connections and support women in entrepreneurship and leadership. In the search for that path, I am choosing patience and grace.

I am reminded of this quote:

"Don't ask what the world needs. Ask what makes you come alive and go do it. Because what the world needs is more people who have come alive."
—Howard Thurman

About the Author

Adrienne Palmer is an accomplished entrepreneur who founded her first technology company in 1998. While leading Insite (insite.net), Adrienne was recognized as one of Dallas' Top Women in Business and amongst the elite North Texas Women in Technology. She was frequently featured in the media for her technology and entrepreneurial achievements. Insite continues to be internationally recognized for its innovative work, receiving top industry awards.

Following the acquisition of Insite in 2016 by a national agency, Adrienne became the Chief Leadership Officer for Skvare (skvare.com) where she grew the team and prepared the company for another successful exit in 2023.

Adrienne held a three-year term as Global Director of Entrepreneurs' Organization (EO, eonetwork.org), chaired the Advisory Board for the Network for Teaching Entrepreneurship (NFTE, nfte.com), and continues to serve as an Advisor to the Global Student Entrepreneur Awards (GSEA, gsea.org).

Adrienne continues to deliver her expertise and guidance as a coach, mentor, and leadership consultant for entrepreneurs. She frequently facilitates diplomatic programs focused on supporting entrepreneurs and their impact in the global economy, including programs of the US State Department, the United Nations, and the World Affairs Council. She also leads the World Citizens Guide (worldcitizensguide.com), a cross-cultural communication movement. Adrienne is committed to supporting and empowering all entrepreneurs, with a personal passion for supporting women entrepreneurs.

In 2024, Adrienne embarked upon an exciting journey of self-discovery and global connection. She and her husband moved full-time aboard a sailboat to explore the world by sea. Adrienne is an experienced, internationally certified skipper who continues mentoring, consulting, and writing as she discovers new facets of herself and the world around her.

Connect with Adrienne:

Connect with Adrienne at adrienne@adriennep.com or visit SailingAmazingGrace.com to learn more of her story.

CHAPTER 7

Forged in Fire

"By embracing gratitude, we find abundance in the present, courage in the unknown, and the power to reshape our journey."
—*Marsha Ralls*

By Marsha Ralls

LIFE HAS A WAY OF SURPRISING US, often when we least expect it. Over the years, I've faced trials that have tested my spirit and resilience. However, through these challenges, I discovered something powerful: the transformative nature of gratitude.

In 2016, I was still grappling with the profound absence left by my mother's passing a few years earlier. Her battle with breast cancer had carved a deep void in my life, and the weight of grief lingered, refusing to ease with time. She had been my anchor, and without her, it felt as if a vital piece of myself had vanished. The sorrow was unrelenting, leaving me adrift in a world that suddenly felt vast and impossible to navigate.

As I was grappling with that loss, life dealt me another blow. I found myself in a situation where I had trusted someone I shouldn't have, which led me into a financial mess. The betrayal hit hard. What was supposed to be an anchor turned out to be a trap, and I felt like my entire world was crumbling around me.

My business, which had once been a source of pride and purpose, began to falter. I fought tirelessly to keep it alive, pouring all my energy into saving what I had built, but it felt like swimming against a powerful current. One setback followed another, and before long, I faced the heartbreaking reality of losing not just my business but also my home of over 25 years, the place where I had raised my two sons. I never had the chance to return to my home or even pack up my belongings. The locks were changed, and I was left with nothing but the weight of memories. Our home, once filled with laughter, love, and life, now felt like a distant chapter, something I could never reclaim.

During this time, I found myself in a dark place, questioning everything. I was diagnosed with PTSD and anxiety, and there were days when I could barely muster the strength to get out of bed. I struggled to find a way forward. This experience was so foreign to me. Before all of this, I had always been able to find joy in everyday life, no matter what was going on around me. I could always find something beautiful happening, something to lift my spirit. But now, it felt like I was lost in a fog, unable to connect with the sense of peace I had once known. Yet, amidst that despair, I began to notice small moments of relief that cut through the heaviness, moments that gave me a glimmer of hope.

I started paying closer attention to the simple things that brought me comfort—the warmth of sunlight on my face, the sound of rain tapping gently on the window, or a friend reaching out to check in on me. Slowly, I realized these small moments held more significance than I had ever given them credit for. It sparked an idea: to create a gratitude journal where I could intentionally look for the good in each day, no matter how small. It helped me focus on the positive, even when things were tough. It was a reminder that there's always something to be thankful for.

I began embracing mindfulness and meditation, intentionally sitting with my feelings. I didn't try to avoid the pain; instead, I created space to honor it while also looking for moments of hope amidst the hardship. The support of my Entrepreneurs' Organization (EO) community became a lifeline. Their empathy and understanding as fellow entrepreneurs reminded me that I wasn't alone, even on the hardest days. As I meditated and connected with others, I discovered a new way of seeing things. This didn't take away the pain or the memories of loss, but it allowed me to acknowledge those emotions while welcoming the good that remained in my life. I recognized the strength and resilience I had developed over the years—an inner power that had carried me through so much, shaping who I am today.

Grief is a tumultuous journey. I soon realized it isn't a straight path; it ebbs and flows, sometimes crashing over me like a relentless wave. The void left by my mother's absence and the loss of my business and my home were profound, but in acknowledging my pain, I also discovered the strength to embrace gratitude. I learned that it's possible to hold sorrow and appreciation in the same breath.

With each step, a quiet transformation began to take root. I came to understand that resilience isn't about being untouched by hardship but rather about rising and finding purpose beyond it. The journey through loss wasn't an end; it sparked a renewal, deepening my understanding of myself and my connection with others. Like many of you may have experienced, resilience isn't loud; it builds with every decision to continue, even when the road ahead is unclear.

Gratitude became my guide through this darkness. Instead of focusing solely on what was gone, it helped me see what still remained. In the smallest moments of grace, I found a way to reclaim my story. By choosing to notice these moments, I drew strength—not by avoiding the pain, but by letting gratitude lead me to a new way of being.

RISING FROM THE ASHES

As I leaned deeper into gratitude, I began to notice a gradual change within myself. It wasn't immediate, but small moments of peace—like a friend's kind words or a quiet minute of reflection—started to pierce through the heaviness of grief. These moments became essential, showing me that gratitude could be more than just an emotion; it could be a signal from the universe, an invitation to healing, growth, and new possibilities.

Seeking to understand this process more fully, I turned to the teachings of Dr. Joe Dispenza. His groundbreaking work in neuroscience revealed the powerful influence emotions like gratitude have on both the mind and the body. Motivated by this insight, I became a certified NeuroChangeSolutions (NCS) consultant, learning how to guide others through similar transformative experiences. With this science-based methodology, I found that gratitude not only helped me build personal resilience but also allowed me to empower others to unlock their own potential for healing and growth.

Gratitude as a State of Readiness

Gratitude is more than a polite response to kindness; it's a profound signal to the universe that we are ready to embrace transformation. Practicing gratitude became a way to prepare myself to receive life's next chapters with an open heart. This readiness was like turning toward the sun each day, allowing warmth and growth to unfold naturally. I began by acknowledging small blessings—a meaningful conversation, a quiet moment outdoors, or even just the feeling of calm in the morning. With each expression of thanks, I felt my capacity for positive change expand, opening doors to new experiences and deeper peace.

Finding Calm and Clarity

Practicing gratitude moves us out of survival mode, helping to quiet stress and bring a sense of harmony and balance to our lives. I remember how a simple morning ritual—reflecting on three things I felt grateful for—had the power to reshape my entire day. Instead of reacting to challenges with anxiety, I found clarity and perseverance. In moments of appreciation, I could feel myself lifting out of the day-to-day pressures and reconnecting to a sense of purpose, setting a foundation for positive, intentional action.

Gratitude's Influence on the Body and Mind

Gratitude doesn't just impact our mental state; it also deeply influences our physical well-being. Research has shown that gratitude can boost immunity and reduce stress, enhancing the body's natural healing abilities. This became particularly evident to me during times of illness and uncertainty when practicing gratitude helped me feel more grounded, stronger, and better equipped to recover. In those moments of genuine appreciation, I could sense a good change in my body's chemistry, reinforcing the profound connection between our emotions and physical health and highlighting the role gratitude plays in fostering resilience and vitality.

The Power of Consistent Gratitude

Gratitude requires intention, but the impact is deeply transformative. By making it a daily practice, I began to break free from thought patterns that had once held me captive. It wasn't always easy, but over time, I noticed a difference in how I perceived situations. Instead of letting challenges overwhelm me, I started to find value in every experience, even the difficult ones. It wasn't a brief remedy; it became a new way of engaging with life. The more I practiced gratitude, the more I felt connected to the world around me, embracing an openness and appreciation for all that I encountered.

Ripple Effect of Gratitude

Gratitude doesn't just change us—it radiates outward, influencing those around us. As I deepened my connection with gratitude, I noticed how it improved my relationships and created a healing and supportive environment. Expressing appreciation for the people in my life inspired something in them—encouraging them to share their own gratitude and extend it to their circles. This created a positive loop where everyone felt uplifted and empowered. The cycle of gratitude not only strengthened my connections but also enriched the lives of those around me, nurturing a collective sense of resilience, hope, and love.

Mastering Emotions Through Gratitude

I feel more in control of my emotional states when I practice gratitude, which inspires me with a more proactive approach to personal transformation. It became clear that I could choose how to respond to life's challenges, and this newfound empowerment ignited a fire within me. No longer a passive observer, I stepped into the role of an active participant in my own story. Gratitude allowed me to reclaim my strength and take charge of my narrative, transforming perceived obstacles into opportunities for growth.

The Journey Continues

Looking back on my path, I am filled with a profound sense of gratitude—not just for the milestones I've achieved but for the lessons I've learned along the way. Each experience, each moment of reflection, has contributed to a richer understanding of what it means to be truly alive. I've come to realize that gratitude is much more than an emotion or reaction; it is a powerful practice that can change our lives in ways we never imagined.

With this understanding, I invite anyone reading this to embrace gratitude as a tool for personal growth. Whether you're navigating a difficult phase in your life or simply seeking to elevate your daily experience, remember that gratitude is always within reach. It lives in the simple moments—the laughter shared with a friend, the beauty of nature, the warmth of a loved one—that we find the seeds of transformation waiting to blossom.

CURATOR OF CHANGE

Gratitude became the foundation of my leadership and how I connect with others. As I integrated it more fully into my life, my priorities naturally shifted—relationships deepened, and my vision for the impact I wanted to create became clearer. What started out as a personal practice evolved into a guiding force, shaping how I led and the energy I brought to every interaction.

Rather than leading from a place of obligation or outcome, I began to approach each moment with a mindset of appreciation, which opened doors for more meaningful collaboration, growth, and resilience. I leaned into each experience with appreciation, finding joy in the journey and inspiring others to do the same. Gratitude allowed me to lead with authenticity and openness, creating an environment where people felt seen, supported, and valued.

Leading Through Authenticity and Vulnerability

Gratitude transformed the way I lead, encouraging me to embrace vulnerability and authenticity. No longer did I feel the need to hide my struggles; I began sharing both my victories and challenges openly. This transparency allowed others to see the whole of my journey—not just the polished successes but the messy, real parts, too. By showing up as my true self, I created an environment where others felt encouraged to be open, too, building a community centered on acceptance and growth.

One of my core intentions was to build a community where women could support each other. Through founding EO Women, I wanted to ensure no woman ever felt alone. This space was designed to provide support, encouragement, and a reminder that we are all part of something greater than ourselves. Sharing my story wasn't always comfortable, but gratitude gave me the courage to take that step. What once felt risky became a chance to inspire others to do the same, reinforcing that every individual's experience is valuable and worthy of recognition.

Building Resilience Through Gratitude

In 2021, amidst the uncertainty of the COVID-19 pandemic, I founded The Phoenix Asheville—a vision brought to life during one of the most challenging times for businesses. The process was daunting, with obstacles at every turn, but I chose to stay grounded in the purpose behind our mission and in the small, steady progress we made each day. This approach helped me stay focused on the long-term goal rather than being consumed by immediate setbacks.

Then, when Hurricane Helene hit Asheville, we were faced with even more hurdles. The storm left widespread devastation, forcing us to cancel all remaining retreats for 2024. Walking through the damage around us, I was reminded of how fragile our plans can be. Yet, despite the destruction, The Phoenix Asheville itself was unharmed, and I found a deep sense of gratitude in this. The catastrophe tested our resilience, but it also highlighted the strength of the community we had built, allowing us to navigate these setbacks and continue moving forward, anchored in our shared goals and values.

Spreading the Ripple Effect of Gratitude

As I embraced gratitude, its influence began to extend far beyond my own journey. Those around me—friends, family, and my community—began to respond differently, as if the energy of appreciation was contagious. When I express my thankfulness, it invites others to recognize the positives in their own lives. A whisper of hope, born from a solitary soul, grew into a chorus of optimism, echoing through a community united in gratitude.

Motivated by this powerful shift, I took action to channel this energy into something tangible. I led a NeuroChangeSolutions workshop in New York City, where all proceeds were directed toward supporting the rebuilding efforts in Asheville. The event was an opportunity to align our intentions and create an impact through shared purpose. The workshop became a platform for transforming our gratitude into action, with every participant contributing to the greater good.

This experience reaffirmed how gratitude, when practiced collectively, becomes a transformative force. It transcended the act of giving, evolving into a unifying force that empowered us to not only rebuild Asheville but also to elevate the collective energy of our community. What began as an individual practice became a shared movement, one that connected us all in the pursuit of resilience and transformation.

Elevating Community and Collaboration

Gratitude changes how we interact and work together. When we focus on appreciating the efforts of others, it strengthens relationships and encourages a team-oriented mindset. People feel more valued, which sparks greater participation and mutual support.

In collaborative settings, gratitude helps us focus not just on the end result but on the growth and effort that led to it. Acknowledging each person's role creates an environment where everyone is motivated to contribute, making teamwork more effective and meaningful.

Guiding My Future with Gratitude

Curating change through gratitude is about taking ownership of how I respond to life's challenges. In challenging situations, I don't wait for change—I make it happen. Each new endeavor becomes an opportunity to inspire, empower, and elevate others, grounding me in the joy of giving rather than receiving.

And in the toughest moments, gratitude reveals the deeper lessons within adversity. I've learned to seek wisdom from hardships, recognizing that each setback carries valuable insight. This mindset helps me stay centered, even when facing overwhelming circumstances. By embracing abundance in the face of difficulty, I'm able to stay focused on progress, knowing that each experience strengthens my resilience and fuels my path forward.

Looking ahead, I carry gratitude with me as I navigate new paths. It's the lens through which I view my goals, relationships, and legacy. With each new challenge or opportunity, it allows me to keep moving forward with intention without losing sight of my core values. I stay focused on how I can impact others and lead by example.

Closing Thoughts

As we conclude this journey through gratitude, I hope the insights shared have sparked a sense of possibility. Gratitude has become my compass, offering resilience through challenges, guiding authentic connections, and building a path shaped by purpose and compassion. Through this practice, I've seen how it strengthens our ability to face adversity, unites us with others, and lights the way forward, not just for ourselves but for everyone we encounter.

If this message resonates or if you're curious about exploring gratitude's transformative power in your own life, I'd love to connect (curatorofchange@gmail.com). Together, we can keep building a ripple of positive change, creating a future where gratitude and purpose are at the heart of everything we do.

About the Author

Marsha Ralls is the Founder and CEO of The Phoenix Asheville, a luxury retreat center located in Asheville, North Carolina. Since its establishment in 2021, Marsha has led The Phoenix with a vision to provide a sanctuary for personal inspiration, growth, and life transformation.

Marsha Ralls brings a diverse background encompassing hospitality, wellness, fine arts, and neuroscience, offering a distinctive blend of expertise to her role. As a NeuroChangeSolutions (NCS) consultant, certified yoga instructor, global speaker, author, and mindfulness coach, she seamlessly integrates her passion for fitness, nature, and service.

Throughout her multifaceted career, Marsha has consistently brought like-minded individuals together to create meaningful impact. Her entrepreneurial spirit has driven her to found and lead various ventures, including serving as the President and CEO of Closed Monday Productions. She also founded the internationally recognized global art advisory group, The Ralls Collection, where she curated over 449 exhibitions with prominent artists, including her mentor, Robert Rauschenberg.

She is a servant leader and dedicated to giving back to her community. Her commitment to community engagement and service is evident in her involvement in the Economic Club of Washington, DC, Entrepreneurs' Organization's and as a Trustee on the Board of Directors of the Blue Ridge Parkway Foundation.

Marsha Ralls continues to inspire—curating change, and elevate consciousness with every endeavor. As the driving force behind The Phoenix Asheville, she empowers individuals to transcend limitations and manifest their fullest potential, creating the life they dream.

Connect with Marsha:

LinkedIn: linkedin.com/in/marsharalls

CHAPTER 8

The Power of Gratitude: A Journey of Empowerment and Transformation

Step into your power, reclaim your vitality,
and create the life you were meant to live.
—**Manon de Veritch**

By Manon de Veritch

STANDING ON THE SHORES OF PUGET SOUND, just a few steps away from my home in Gig Harbor, Washington, I often reflect with humility on the unexpected journey that brought me here. I hadn't set out to be an entrepreneur or technologist, let alone an energy healer and mentor. But our lives have a way of presenting people, opportunities, and signs that we need only be

A JOURNEY OF EMPOWERMENT AND TRANSFORMATION

open to hearing, feeling, and trusting that what we seek is seeking us.

Today, I lead two thriving businesses, each born from a passion for empowerment and transformation. Nuvalo, the company I founded over 15 years ago, is a trusted partner to IT executives, helping them plan and execute complex technology initiatives with clarity and confidence. More recently, I launched Aligned Energy Medicine, a holistic wellness practice focused on transformational healing through sound, light, and frequency. Both ventures, though seemingly different, share a common purpose: to empower individuals and organizations to recognize their power, align with their purpose, and realize their highest potential. My path has been one of growth, resilience, and an unwavering belief in the energy of possibility—and it is gratitude that has illuminated the way.

Gratitude has become more than just a practice; it is the lens through which I view every experience, every challenge, and every triumph. It is a force that has transformed not only my life but also the lives of those I serve, from IT executives navigating the complexities of digital transformation to women reclaiming their inner power through energy medicine. I see it now as energy, frequency, and vibration.

A Foundation in Empowerment

My entrepreneurial journey began with a simple yet profound question: How could I empower others? Fresh out of UC Santa Barbara, I started my Silicon Valley career in technology sales, immersing myself in the fast-paced world of telecommunications, data centers, and Internet infrastructure. By the time I joined Qwest Communications, I had sold nearly every service that corporate IT departments purchase, gaining firsthand insight into the complexities and inefficiencies of both the buyers and sellers of technology products and services.

When the 2008 recession hit, I faced a pivotal choice: stay in the Bay Area and weather the storm or accept a relocation package to Seattle. Choosing the latter, my family moved to Gig Harbor, a picturesque town that would become the backdrop for my personal and professional transformation.

In 2010, I founded Nuvalo with a vision to act as a next-generation channel partner, bridging the gap between buyers and sellers of emerging technologies. I wanted to empower IT

A JOURNEY OF EMPOWERMENT AND TRANSFORMATION

executives to make informed decisions, free from the biases and limitations of traditional supplier relationships. Over the past 15 years, Nuvalo has evolved alongside the IT landscape, helping organizations unlock opportunities in cloud computing, unified communications, cybersecurity, artificial intelligence, and beyond.

As my business acumen and client base grew, so did my understanding of empowerment. I realized it wasn't just about educating and offering tools and resources; it was about helping executives see their own potential, make confident decisions, and take ownership of their futures well beyond their offices. Gratitude played a critical role in this process, grounding me in the belief that every challenge was an opportunity to learn and grow. I consciously expanded my advisory role beyond technology to encompass a more holistic approach to leadership, impact, and influence.

It was at this time that I was introduced by my business coach, Dr. Amelia Case, to the roles energy and intention play in business, relationships, and life in general. I am forever grateful to Amelia for distilling decades of immense business and interpersonal mastery into subtle shifts and bigger wins that were far more heart-centered and fulfilling for me and my clients. She taught me that all of our experiences build on each other. Nothing in nature is wasted. When it came time to launch Aligned Energy Medicine, I was grateful for the reminder that I was not building from scratch; I would parlay my experience with infrastructure and operations, sales and marketing, and public speaking to swiftly lay the foundation for an integrative holistic wellness center.

The Wake-Up Call

By 2018, Nuvalo was a seven-figure technology start-up that had grown from a one-person IT brokerage to an international cloud advisory with three lines of business and employees in five states. I was traveling every other week to visit clients, employees, and partners and attend conferences. I was a recurring speaker and panelist at industry summits and the co-founder and CFO of Cloud Girls, a nonprofit dedicated to educating, mentoring, and giving back to the next generation of women in tech. I was at the top of my game, excelling by all accounts in a primarily male-driven industry and still finding time to raise two vibrant and athletic boys. I was addicted to the adrenaline rush and didn't remember life being any other way than pedal-to-the-metal. I think most career women are sucked into this lifestyle and

A JOURNEY OF EMPOWERMENT AND TRANSFORMATION

rationalize the cortisol rush as a way to drive focus and productivity. Because "workism" (Derek Thompson's phrase to depict work as the centerpiece of one's identity and life's purpose) is so rampant in our culture, the physical, emotional, and chemical effects of stress are largely normalized and ignored.

Despite my professional success, the demands of "workism" began to take a toll. For decades, I had lived by a code that equated worth with productivity, believing that struggle was a necessary price for achievement. By my mid-40s, my body was breaking down. I was exhausted, overextended, and disconnected from my inner self.

There comes a point in our lives when our lifestyles catch up with us, and our bodies, which were never designed for years of sustained stress, go from nudging and nagging to shouting at us and then straight up failing. I didn't have the words or perspective at the time, but it became very clear that how I was living was no longer working for me personally or professionally.

For starters, my hormones were so imbalanced that my doctor was surprised I could even get out of bed. I was in adrenal shutdown and had been surviving on my constitution alone. She said something that struck me so deeply that it is now woven into my mission. She said, "I'll bet you don't even remember what joy feels like. I'm going to help you remember." I believe that certain souls come into our lives at the precise moment we need them, and it's up to us to recognize those synchronicities for the miracles that they are. Think about it: Are there moments in your life when you've actually felt the most simply stated words deep in your core? Maybe it literally created a shockwave of energy through your body, or you seemed to take a picture of the precise moment in time as if it were being catalogued? However you experienced the "a-ha" moment, you knew it was important. That was my experience in Dr. Tami's office.

My work with Dr. Tami Meraglia was the catalyst for my journey to vitality and personal transformation. Not only did she help me physically and chemically, but she also introduced me to meditation, frequency, and the laws of quantum physics, which I consider to be the science behind spirituality. Dr. Tami also taught me to be the CEO of my own body. In a world where we have been conditioned to blindly trust and follow anyone in a white coat, she recognizes the power of our own inner wisdom and agency. Wellness practitioners should be considered advisors and advocates, each bringing their unique experiences and

A JOURNEY OF EMPOWERMENT AND TRANSFORMATION

perspectives to your Board of Advisors. Ultimately, we should exercise our free will to choose what feels aligned with our inner wisdom and truth.

In the years that followed, I experienced what I have come to call a spiritual awakening. Chance conversations and messages from strangers opened the doors to numerous healers, teachers, and retreats, which seemed to line up at the perfect time. I began to notice how my body was responding somatically with either chills and enthusiasm or repulsion. I would follow breadcrumbs from shows, ads, and anything that seemed to be presenting itself repeatedly, booking expensive trips with zero hesitation that the time and money would line up. What has proven the most important "yes" to date was my decision to embark on a nine-month Vision Quest with two extraordinary shamans, Kanaychowa and Desoweno. These amazing women have now led me through three Vision Quests, deepening my work with earth and astral energies and becoming clear on who I am and why I'm here. I cannot recommend this journey strongly enough to anyone at an inflection point.

I had never considered myself a religious or spiritual person growing up. I had a very "Dana Scully" way of thinking about the world, needing to see to believe or have data as proof. Now, I was in the midst of my own experiential education, feeling and influencing energy, and receiving intuitive guidance that resonates as truth. This journey into the world of energy and quantum physics (sub-atomic energy) marked a profound turning point, allowing me to reconnect with and trust my inner wisdom and see the bigger picture of my life's purpose.

For the first time, I began to view my body not as a machine to be optimized but as an energetic being with an innate capacity for healing. Through gratitude, I embraced the teachers, lessons, and angels in human and spirit form who appeared along the way, guiding me toward a new understanding of health, alignment, and self-sovereignty.

Building Aligned Energy Medicine

In 2021, I felt the calling to extend my work beyond the corporate world. I founded Aligned Energy Medicine to help others navigate their journeys of healing and transformation. Energy is our life force; it animates every living being. It flows through and sustains every aspect of life, from physical vitality to mental and emotional well-being. Energy Medicine (or

A JOURNEY OF EMPOWERMENT AND TRANSFORMATION

Vibrational Medicine) tends to this life force. Some increasingly popular energy medicine modalities include Reiki, Biofield Tuning, sound healing, acupuncture, reflexology, Qigong, yoga, and somatic breathwork. Despite being relatively new to Americans, they have been practiced for thousands of years.

While I work with men and women of all ages, my clients are primarily working women in their 40s and 50s, who, like me, have spent years prioritizing others and carrying huge responsibilities while neglecting their own needs. Many are stuck in careers or relationships that no longer serve them, and they want to reclaim joy, passion, and aliveness. They realize that promotions, wealth, and material possessions no longer motivate them, as they seek fulfillment and purpose on a more spiritual level.

Whether they come in for energy healing, Erotic Blueprint™ coaching, or 6-12 month mentorships, I use a combination of modalities to dissolve inner conflict, clear emotional knots, and resolve stored trauma, allowing the nervous system to reset and the body to harmonize and heal. Together, we reconnect with their inner wisdom and life force energy, kundalini energy, and sexual energy, clearing out energies that are not serving them, including patterns, traumas, and limiting beliefs.

Living in alignment with your purpose means consciously making decisions and taking actions that are in line with your deepest values, passions, and what you believe gives your life meaning. I believe that when we live in alignment with our soul's purpose, whether that is your career, passion project, or simply radiating love and compassion, you and life as you experience it will happen with flow and ease. Synchronicities abound. Dreams manifest. Open-heartedness and gratitude preside. If you have ever experienced this state, it becomes very obvious when you fall "out" of alignment, and with practice, you will more quickly and easily return to flow.

Through one-on-one sessions, workshops, and retreats, I help men and women reconnect with their inner healer, clear limiting beliefs, and awaken to their true power and potential. Gratitude is a cornerstone of this work, reminding us that every experience—no matter how painful—carries a gift, and by harnessing the frequency of gratitude, you are the creator of your life.

A JOURNEY OF EMPOWERMENT
AND TRANSFORMATION

Conclusion: Gratitude and the Energy of Possibility

As I look back on my journey—from navigating the corporate tech world to founding Nuvalo and now Aligned Energy Medicine—I see how gratitude has been a constant, transformative force. Gratitude shifted my perspective from one of longing and striving to one of abundance and receiving. It taught me that everything I've ever experienced, every setback and triumph, has prepared me for this exact moment.

Tony Robbins has an abundance of powerful and thought-provoking quotes I internally recite. One of the most impactful to me is, *"What if everything you've ever experienced has prepared you for this moment?"* Those words are etched in my heart, a mantra that affirms the interconnectedness of all things. Every challenge, every teacher, every serendipitous encounter has been part of a divine blueprint, aligning me with my dharma to serve, empower, and uplift.

Dr. David Hawkins' scale of consciousness has been a profound guide in my understanding of gratitude. His second law of thermodynamics speaks to the energy inherent in emotions, and gratitude ranks among the highest frequencies. When we operate from gratitude, we vibrate not from a place of lack—of wanting—but from a place of having. Gratitude amplifies the energy of what *already is*, creating a fertile ground for manifesting our greatest potential.

One of Dr. Joe Dispenza's most powerful teachings is, "Gratitude is the ultimate state of receivership." This beautifully summarizes his science-driven explanations of how we send a thought out (e.g., what we want to manifest, such as health, wealth, or relationships) and call it back to us via the emotion of gratitude (implying we have it already). We continue to receive more of what we are grateful for, so act as if it's already yours.

I've learned that empowerment and self-sovereignty begin with recognizing our own energy and its infinite capacity. By reconnecting with our inner wisdom, we remember that the answers we seek are not outside us but within. Gratitude becomes the bridge between our inner healer and the life we wish to create.

The irony of my journey is not lost on me. Once again, I find myself at the forefront of a paradigm shift, helping people make sense of a concept that many find abstract and intangible: energy. Just as I once demystified "Cloud" for IT leaders, I

A JOURNEY OF EMPOWERMENT AND TRANSFORMATION

now guide people to understand how energy, frequency, and intention influence their miraculous ability to heal, transform, and thrive. Soon, people will use energy medicine as their primary means of mitigating physical, emotional, and mental disease, and western medicine as we know it will be the fallback. Like our adoption of smartphones, email, and Zoom meetings, we will wonder how we ever managed without an awareness of and relationship with energy!

Today, I wake up with immense gratitude—not only for the successes and milestones but for the struggles that have shaped me, the teachers who have guided me, and the clients who trust me to walk alongside them on their journeys. Gratitude is more than an emotion; it is a state of being, a frequency that aligns us with our highest potential.

In embodying this truth, I am deeply fulfilled by my work at Aligned Energy Medicine and Nuvalo. Through these ventures, I help others reclaim their agency, reconnect with their purpose, and realize their limitless potential. Gratitude is not just part of my story; it is the force that has written every chapter, connecting each seemingly disparate piece into a coherent, beautiful whole.

As I continue on this journey, I envision a world where more of us operate from the energy of gratitude—heart-centered, empowered, self-sovereign, and vibrationally aligned with our most authentic and truest selves. What a world that will be.

A JOURNEY OF EMPOWERMENT
AND TRANSFORMATION

About the Author

Manon de Veritch is a distinguished technology executive, entrepreneur, and passionate advocate of vibrational medicine, blending her vast corporate experience with a deep commitment to healing and self-empowerment. Once a guide for executives navigating the Cloud revolution, Manon now helps individuals harness the science and life-changing impact of energy healing to reclaim their health, vitality, and personal sovereignty.

Manon's own journey from burnout to purpose fuels her mission to inspire others to align with their highest potential. As a certified energy medicine practitioner and Erotic Blueprint™ coach, her work is rooted in the belief that we are electromagnetic beings with the innate ability to heal ourselves. By reconnecting with the body's energy using sound, light, frequency, and intention, she empowers clients to release blocks, reverse illness, and restore inner harmony.

Manon's framework for holistic wellness blends ancient energy healing practices like Reiki and sound therapy with psychospiritual techniques to dissolve limiting beliefs, patterns, and traumas at their source. Her transformative mentorships and personalized sessions guide individuals to break free from pain, re-write their story, and live with passion and purpose.

Whether through personalized sessions or transformative mentorships, Manon invites you to step into your power, reclaim your vitality, and create the life you were meant to live.

Connect with Manon:

www.linkedin.com/in/manondeveritch

CEO, Nuvalo: www.nuvalo.com

CEO, Aligned Energy Medicine: www.alignedenergymedicine.com

CHAPTER 9

Gratitude & Grace

"My leadership is rooted in gratitude for those who paved the way and a commitment to lift others with grace and purpose."

By Amy Boone Thompson

IT WAS 1995, AND I HAD JUST GRADUATED from George Mason University as a student-athlete. I was working as both an assistant strength coach and a personal trainer while putting myself through sports massage therapy school. My first job as a personal trainer was at The Women's Club of Chantilly, VA. I was eager and excited to apply everything I'd learned and willing to put in the work. Because of that willingness and a genuine desire to connect with people, my business grew quickly. Simply by being present, consistent, and building relationships, I earned the trust of my clients, one session at a time.

The best memories I carry from that first job aren't just about skills or techniques. They're about the clients I trained, the women who trusted me to guide them in their fitness and wellness journeys. I keep a book of their profiles, pictures, and success stories—a collection of moments that, even years later, continue to inspire me. These clients were more than just people I trained. They were resilient, hopeful, and open, each of them showing up day after day to work toward their goals. Their determination reminded me, over and over, of the impact a fitness professional could have on someone's life. They became my "why," my purpose, and the reason I knew I belonged in this industry.

That experience, those clients, and the stories we created together were what solidified my path in the health and wellness industry. It was more than a job; it was the beginning of my understanding that fitness is about connection, resilience, and empowerment. And it's why, to this day, I'm so committed to supporting others in their wellness journeys. I know firsthand the lasting impact one fitness professional can have, not just on a client's physical health but on their confidence, mindset, and overall life. This is my story, and I know it's one that resonates with so many others in our field. Most of us have that first client or that first job where we realize we're not just teaching movement; we're making a difference.

Decades later, as I found myself in a different chapter—leading IDEA® Health and Fitness Association through a turbulent period for our industry—the lessons from those early days grounded me. I'd spent years as IDEA's VP and GM, guiding it through the pandemic and witnessing firsthand the challenges that fitness professionals and business owners were facing. When the opportunity came to purchase IDEA, I knew exactly what I was taking on and jumped at the opportunity. I understood the roadblocks, the market shifts, and the uphill climb that lay ahead. But I also knew the potential, the legacy, and the power of IDEA's platform, because it had been such an integral part of my own journey.

In many ways, stepping into ownership of IDEA was like reconnecting with my roots. It brought me back to those days in Chantilly when I saw how a single trainer could inspire, uplift, and change lives. Owning IDEA meant I could support thousands of professionals like that, each of them out there making a difference. But as exciting as this opportunity was, it came with an array of challenges I had never faced before.

The transition was difficult, and the initial hurdles were steep. Operational challenges, financial pressures, and the evolving needs of the industry created an environment where there was no room for shortcuts. Every day brought a new, often overwhelming decision to make. But in those moments, I found myself turning back to the same tool that had sustained me all these years: GRATITUDE. Instead of letting the weight of the challenges pull me under, I leaned into the lessons each one offered. I reminded myself of those first clients, the trust they placed in me, and the purpose they instilled in me. Each challenge became an opportunity to grow, not just the business but also myself as a leader.

Gratitude, I've learned, is more than just looking for the positives. It's a shift in perspective that allows us to see challenges as essential parts of growth. When I reframed the difficulties with IDEA, I found myself better equipped to approach each problem with clarity and openness. Gratitude helped me see that every setback, every roadblock, was a stepping stone for building a stronger, more resilient organization, and in choosing gratitude, I found not only my own resilience but a renewed sense of purpose that I could share with my team.

That same gratitude also taught me the importance of leading with grace, especially in uncertain times. Grace, for me, is about empathy, humility, and the willingness to keep learning—even when there's no clear answer. It meant giving my team and myself permission to try, fail, and try again. I encouraged a culture where we could be open about our challenges, confident that setbacks were simply part of our journey. Grace allowed me to support my team without expecting perfection, creating an environment where they felt safe to experiment and grow.

Throughout this process, I discovered a new level of resilience, one that goes beyond simply pushing through hard times. Resilience, I realized, is about adapting, evolving, and finding new perspectives on challenges. It's about holding on to the vision, even if the path to it isn't what you'd originally planned. Gratitude played a fundamental role in that resilience, and by embracing gratitude for the lessons in each hardship, I learned to navigate the journey with a lighter heart. This, in turn, allowed me to inspire and support others in their own moments of struggle.

There were days when the way forward wasn't clear, and the obstacles seemed larger than the vision. But in those moments, I'd remind myself of my own journey and the stories of those first clients who inspired me to keep going. Resilience, I realized, isn't about never feeling doubt; it's about embracing that doubt with gratitude and moving forward anyway. By sharing this approach openly with my team, I fostered a sense of patience, persistence, and mutual support. Together, we began to see setbacks not as failures but as opportunities to recalibrate, refine, and strengthen our strategies.

Leading IDEA also taught me that courage is essential for authentic leadership. True courage doesn't come from always projecting strength. Instead, it's about being honest about the uncertainties, willing to learn, and showing vulnerability. As I navigated the unknowns of ownership, I found that my willingness to be open with my team created a deeper connection. They saw that leadership wasn't about having all the answers but about being present, adaptable, and committed to growth.

This openness helped foster a culture of innovation, trust, and psychological safety within the company. By sharing my challenges, I invited my team to embrace their own courage and resilience, creating an environment where everyone felt empowered to contribute fully. Through this journey, I've come to see that resilience and vulnerability can coexist beautifully. They're not opposites; they're partners in creating authentic leadership.

For me, gratitude and grace are not just ideas—they're practices I work to cultivate every day. A daily moment of reflection helps me find something positive to anchor my mindset each morning. This simple ritual has a profound effect, setting a tone of clarity and calm that sustains me through each day.

I also lean on my support network of people who inspire, challenge, and uplift me. Connecting with other women leaders reminds me of our shared experiences and the strength we find in each other. Self-compassion has been equally important. It's easy to be your own harshest critic, but I've learned that giving myself grace in moments of struggle allows me to lead with resilience without the weight of self-doubt.

Finally, mentorship has become a way for me to pay forward my gratitude for my journey while supporting others on their individual paths. At IDEA, we have implemented a formal mentorship program where we provide a structured and guided platform to support emerging and experienced professionals at every stage of their careers. This program reminds me that our impact as leaders reaches beyond our immediate circle—it's a ripple that can uplift others.

Ultimately, every challenge has become a building block for a resilient, impactful career. Through gratitude, grace, and resilience, women in leadership can create a legacy that inspires others to approach challenges with openness and courage. My message to women leaders is clear: By valuing each step of the journey, including the tough parts, we can create a path that uplifts others and paves the way for lasting change.

About the Author

"With gratitude for every step of the journey and grace in every decision, I embody the power of fitness as a force for positive change."

"Through gratitude and grace, true strength lies not only in our bodies but in our ability to empower others along the way."

Connect with Amy:

Instagram: @amyboonethompson

IDEA Health & Fitness Association
LinkedIn: linkedin.com/company/idea-health-&-fitness
Instagram: @ideafit

CEO, IDEAfit, Inc
www.ideafit.com

CEO, IDEAfit Insurance Services
https://ideafitinsuranceservices.com

CHAPTER 10

From Chaos to Calm: A Gratitude Journey

Gratitude is the bridge between what you have and the endless opportunities waiting to flow into your life.

By Daniella Menachemson

MOVING TO A NEW CONTINENT for the third time in my life was an adventure that brought equal parts excitement and uncertainty. This time, my family and I crossed the ocean with 13 suitcases and our beloved dog, LC, ready to start fresh. Little did we know that shortly after arriving in our new home, the world would come to a standstill. COVID-19 broke out, and the hospitality industry, the very foundation of the business I had moved for, was effectively shut down. The timing felt cruel, as if I had leapt off a cliff and was now suspended in free fall. That feeling that everything was falling apart is a theme and often a reminder that you are going in the right direction. It's never apparent at the time, and we never truly have the insight of what's to come.

When you find yourself in an uncomfortable life situation, know that it's there to push you in the direction you are meant to head. Not all storms come to destroy you; some come to clear the path for you.

Yet even in the depths of uncertainty, there was an inner knowing that something bigger was at play. Rather than succumbing to fear, I began to ask myself questions that would change the trajectory of my life: *What are you here to teach me? How can I grow into a better version of myself through this challenge? How can I align and find coherence to recognize the blessings that surround me, even in the midst of chaos?*

The answers to these questions revealed themselves slowly through a journey of stillness, reflection, and, ultimately, gratitude.

The Lifequake

Before I even arrived in this new chapter of life, I experienced what I now call a "lifequake." In August 2019, I went through a devastating exit from a family business, an experience that felt like a divorce. The betrayal and loss shattered me, leaving me with a profound sense of failure and uncertainty about how I would rebuild my life. My relationship with my parents, something I held most dear, was suddenly severed. My faith in everything I cherished was deeply shaken.

After getting off a flight and realizing I had been fired from the family business I had spent a large part of my life working in, I was overcome with a profound sense of displacement. The realization that I was dispensable hit hard. It wasn't just about losing a job; it was about losing my identity and questioning where I belonged. At the height of the trauma, I had no idea things were unfolding *for* me and not happening *to me*. At the time, my purpose felt completely unclear, and I was in full fight-or-flight mode, trying to make sense of what had happened.

The anxiety was relentless. I lived with a constant feeling of nausea, questioning how I could possibly rebuild my sense of self and support my family. At the time, it felt as though everything was crumbling. Yet, looking back, I now understand that life doesn't happen *to* us; it happens *for* us. This "lifequake" was a catalyst, pushing me to evolve in ways I couldn't have imagined. It taught me that when everything is stripped away, you are left with the raw materials to rebuild something entirely new and often better.

The Gift of Stillness

As the world paused, I found an unexpected blessing in the stillness that COVID forced upon us. For the first time in years, I had the opportunity to look inward, to pause the frenetic pace of life and focus on healing the parts of myself that felt fractured. The stillness became a mirror, reflecting back the areas in my life where I had been operating from a place of survival rather than alignment. It was during this time that I began to understand the true essence of gratitude.

Stillness brought clarity. I realized how much of my energy had been tied to external validation and the opinions of others. The pause allowed me to ask myself fundamental questions: *What truly matters? What do I value? What kind of life do I want to create?* These reflections shifted my focus from what I had lost to what I still had and could build anew. The power of gratitude began to emerge not as a fleeting thought but as a transformative way of being.

It's always after the fact that you realize what the gift truly was, and that really is the learning: understanding the moments that stand right in front of us and how to appreciate them rather than look past them or take them for granted. During this time, my daily habit of meditation saved me. It provided a structure and a way to process the chaos. Meditation became my anchor, a daily ritual that allowed me to quiet the noise and reconnect with myself. Through this practice, I could sit with my emotions, however difficult they might be, and gradually transform them into something positive.

Gratitude, I realized, is not simply a thought or a polite acknowledgment of good fortune. It is an energetic state, a feeling that arises when your thoughts align with the emotions of your heart. Thinking about gratitude without feeling it is like placing an order at a restaurant and never telling the waitress what you actually want or leaving an email in your drafts folder never to be sent. It was through this realization that I began to cultivate a deeper connection with gratitude, not as a concept but as a way of being.

The Practice of Gratitude

In my search for healing and alignment, I turned to the teachings of Dr. Joe Dispenza. His meditations became the cornerstone of my daily practice, guiding me to shift from a state of flux to a state of flow.

Morning Meditation

Each morning, while my brain was still in an alpha state—calm and receptive—I began my day with Dr. Joe's morning meditation. The practice focused on visualizing my future, replacing repetitive memories of the past with a vivid picture of the life I aspired to create. The key, I learned, was to move beyond thought and into feeling. I didn't just imagine my future; I felt it. I allowed myself to experience gratitude and joy as if my dreams had already come true.

This practice taught me that the goal isn't just to think about gratitude but to embody it. By teaching my body what my future felt like through elevated emotions, I aligned my energy with the life I was creating. Every morning, this meditation became a ritual of renewal, shifting me into a new state of being and setting the tone for my day.

Evening Reflection

At the end of each day, I engaged in the evening meditation, a time for reflection and review. This practice invited me to look back on my day with honesty and grace: *Did I stay conscious and present, or did I fall into unconscious patterns? How could I do better tomorrow? What went well today, and what can I celebrate?*

By ending each day with a focus on gratitude for the moments that went well and an intention to grow, I began to shift my perspective. Challenges became opportunities for growth, and even the smallest blessings felt significant. Those evening reflections helped me to end each day with a sense of peace and accomplishment, no matter what challenges I had faced.

The Transformation

For eight weeks, I committed to these practices, meditating every morning and evening. Slowly but surely, I began to notice profound changes. The anxiety that had once felt overwhelming started to dissipate. The constant feeling of unease and uncertainty gave way to a sense of calm and alignment. By focusing on gratitude and embodying elevated emotions, I transformed not only my energy but also my outlook on life.

What others saw as a catastrophe—the disruption and isolation of COVID—became, for me, a time of renewal and growth. Gratitude became the lens through which I viewed my world, allowing me to see blessings where I once saw challenges. By appreciating the people, opportunities, and moments around me, I fundamentally changed the way I looked at everything.

Moving across the world during a global crisis could have made me curl up into a ball and not get out of bed, but it's not in my DNA to crumble during a crisis. Instead of focusing on the news and allowing doubt to consume me, I chose to look within. From a business perspective, the shutdown gave me an opportunity to focus on the culture and values of the company I wanted to build. Those foundations became imperative in shaping the company into what it is today.

It was also a challenging time for my family. My children were new to a country, trying to integrate and make friends, yet doing so from behind computer screens on Zoom. To this day, they still dislike Zoom meetings and much prefer in-person learning. However, the time at home brought unexpected blessings. We spent time cooking together, taking lunchtime walks, and enjoying continuous movie nights. These moments allowed us to simply *be* together and focus on the positives rather than the negatives around us. It reinforced the importance of connection and family amidst uncertainty.

I also learned the power of setting intentions for the future. I would often write down what I wanted for my family, not as goals but as feelings. I visualized joy, connection, and gratitude as constants in our home. This practice became a guiding principle, reminding me to focus on the emotional outcomes rather than external metrics of success.

Lessons on Gratitude

This journey taught me that gratitude is not merely a thought; it is a state of being. When we align our thoughts with elevated emotions like joy, appreciation, and gratitude, we shift our energy and open ourselves to new possibilities. Here are the key lessons I learned:

- **Gratitude is Energetic Alignment.** Without feeling the emotion, a thought is incomplete. It's the alignment of thought and emotion that creates true gratitude and brings positive life experiences to you.

- **Stillness is an Opportunity.** When life forces you to pause, take the time to reflect and recalibrate. Stillness can be a powerful teacher.

- **Elevating Your State Changes Everything.** By consciously shifting your emotional state, you can transform your perspective and your reality and find joy in the amazing things you already have in your life.

- **Shift Your Lens, Change Your Life.** When you change the way you look at something, the things you look at change without question.

Expanding the Practice of Gratitude

Over time, I began to apply the principles of gratitude beyond my personal meditations. Gratitude became the foundation for how I approached my work, my relationships, and my daily interactions.

In Leadership

In my business, I lead a team of incredible women who inspire and challenge me daily. Gratitude has transformed the way I engage with my team. Rather than focusing solely on outcomes, I began to celebrate the efforts and contributions of each individual. A simple "thank you" or acknowledgment of someone's work creates an environment of mutual respect and motivation. Gratitude fosters connection and builds resilience, both individually and collectively.

In Family Life

As a parent, gratitude deepened my relationship with my children in ways I hadn't fully appreciated before. They became my greatest teachers, showing me the importance of presence and perspective. I learned to cherish the small, imperfect moments: a shared laugh over something silly, dancing wildly together to our favorite songs in the kitchen, a heartfelt conversation during a quiet evening, or even an unexpected hug at the most random times. Of course, there were still the inevitable meltdowns about who had been sneaking into whose closet or whose turn it was to choose the movie, take the trash out, and, yes, unload the dishwasher. But even those chaotic moments became part of the tapestry of our bond, teaching me patience and reminding me that love and connection are often found in the messy, unpolished realities of life.

In Everyday Moments

Gratitude also shifted the way I approached the simple, everyday aspects of life. The routine transformed into something meaningful when viewed through the lens of appreciation. Morning sunlight streaming through the window became a reminder of warmth and renewal. Sipping a cup of coffee underneath its golden rays turned into a grounding ritual, a moment to pause and center myself. A kind word from the people we work with carried unexpected weight and fostered a sense of connection and appreciation. Acts of service, like donating furniture through our company to those in need, became a source of profound gratitude. Knowing that our contributions could bring comfort to someone else added depth and purpose to my everyday life. I found joy in the small details that I had once overlooked, and these seemingly ordinary moments became sources of calm, comfort, and gratitude in an otherwise chaotic world.

The Ripple Effect

Gratitude is not a solitary practice; its impact ripples outward. By changing my energy, I began to influence those around me in profound ways. My team thrived in an environment of positivity, where appreciation and encouragement became the norm. This cultural shift not only enhanced productivity but also deepened our collective sense of purpose and connection. Changing our energy to one of gratitude changes everything. It is impossible to feel hate, jealousy, or negative emotions with a grateful heart. Gratitude creates space for growth, healing, and profound transformation, shaping not just individuals but entire communities. As I reflect on this journey, I am reminded that gratitude is not just a practice; it is a way of life that redefines how we see the world and our place within it.

In my personal life, the ripple effect of gratitude was equally powerful. Family relationships became more harmonious as gratitude fostered understanding and patience. Small gestures of appreciation, like a kind word, created an atmosphere of mutual respect and love.

Even beyond my immediate circles, I began to notice how practicing gratitude inspired others. Acts of service, through my company, to those in need sparked similar generosity in others, creating a chain reaction of kindness. Gratitude proved to be a force that not only enriched my own life but also elevated the lives of those around me, demonstrating its incredible potential to transform communities and connections.

Gratitude is more than a practice; it is a profound way of being. A grateful heart transforms how we experience the world, replacing negativity with appreciation and fostering connection where there was once division. It teaches us that even in the midst of chaos, there is beauty to be found and lessons to be embraced.

Gratitude doesn't just change the moments we live, it changes the lives we touch, creating ripples of positivity that extend far beyond ourselves.

About the Author

Daniella Menachemson is a highly regarded entrepreneur in custom hospitality furniture manufacturing. With a career spanning over two decades, she has become a respected figure in the industry, delivering hotel projects that stand the test of time while adapting to evolving consumer demands.

As an award-winning entrepreneur and leader, Daniella's commitment to excellence has shaped her business and set a high standard for leadership and innovation. Her companies projects reflect her passion for creating environments that are both beautiful and purposeful, embodying her dedication to craftsmanship and forward-thinking approaches.

Beyond her professional achievements, Daniella is a dedicated advocate for personal growth and resilience. Her journey is a testament to the transformative power of gratitude, as she has navigated life's challenges with grace and determination, emerging stronger and more aligned with her purpose. Through her story, she inspires others to find strength in adversity and to embrace the lessons life offers with an open heart.

Whether leading her team, collaborating with clients, or speaking on the power of gratitude, Daniella's unwavering commitment to authenticity and innovation continues to leave a lasting impact on all who encounter her work.

Connect with Daniella:

Instagram: stylenations

Email: daniella@stylenations.com

LinkedIn: daniellamenachemson

CHAPTER 11

Two Sides of Gratitude (Or, Learning to Love My Critter Brain)

By Cheryl Farr

"Gratitude and grief are soulmates, sparring partners, and co-conspirators. They grow our hearts into a greater capacity for joy, empathy, and resilience."

— Brené Brown in *Atlas of the Heart: Mapping Meaningful Connection and the Language of Human Experience*

I have a complicated relationship with gratitude. That may seem like an odd thing to say; it does to me, and I'm the one who said it.

TWO SIDES OF GRATITUDE
(OR, LEARNING TO LOVE MY CRITTER BRAIN)

I love the feeling of being grateful. I love showing my gratitude to others. I know, in my heart of hearts, that gratitude begets joy and happiness and love and fulfillment—all emotions that I love to bask in. And I'm generally a glass-is-half-full kind of person; I like seeing the good in people and in situations.

But everything has a light side and a dark side—and gratitude is no different. Many of the things that I am thankful for in my life were born from experiences that left scars on my heart. And the strengths that I've developed in response are also my Achilles heels.

The Upside

I'm grateful to be blessed with many gifts that have allowed me to have a thriving business that I love. I am an accomplished brand strategist with my own brand consulting firm, SIGNAL Brand Innovation, which has been going strong for more than 15 years. I love having regular opportunities to help C-suite leaders—many of whom are facing complex business and marketplace challenges—align their brands with their business strategy so their organizations can take their next great leap forward.

Before branding, I spent many years as a professional travel writer, which surveys say is the second-most coveted profession in the world (after "rock star"). For years, I wrote guidebooks and magazine articles about destinations like New York City, Hawaii, and Mexico. Earlier, at age 19, I came as close to being a "rock star" as a non-musician can get when I landed a job at Geffen Records on Sunset Boulevard in Los Angeles. I spent three magical years working at one of the coolest record labels in the country with artists like Guns 'n' Roses, Peter Gabriel, Aerosmith, and XTC.

Originally from New Jersey, I left home at 18 and have lived all over the country in the decades since. I spent exciting years living in New York City and Los Angeles. I've lived in majestic Colorado and bucolic Kentucky, by the beaches of Florida and the lakes of Wisconsin. I currently live in Palm Springs, California, a desert wonderland that's also a midcentury modern architectural mecca. I love it here.

I've been married twice—the first time for just over 20 years, and now for 12 and counting. I have two lovely, well-adjusted stepdaughters who I'm proud of and happy to have in my life.

TWO SIDES OF GRATITUDE
(OR, LEARNING TO LOVE MY CRITTER BRAIN)

My life has not sucked—far from it. And I'm grateful for that.

So, what are the gifts that have helped me enjoy such a rich and exciting life, exactly?

I am a survivor. I'm stoic in difficult circumstances and resilient when life takes a bad turn. I can navigate change well. I adapt to new circumstances easily, I can pivot on a dime, and even failure or loss won't keep me down. Twice—at the ages of 18 and 43—I started over with nothing and built a whole new life for myself. Then, at the age of 49, my business fell apart due to a bad merger, and I rebuilt it from scratch.

I'm smart and love to learn. I have a bachelor's degree in history from Arizona State University, a master's degree in history from Columbia University, and an MBA-equivalent Master of Management in Hospitality (MMH) from Cornell University. I didn't go to college at all until I was 23 years old, and I paid for it all on my own.

I am independent in practice and mind. I can support myself, and I'm the primary breadwinner in my family. I have strong opinions, and I'm willing to take the road less traveled.

I am committed and tenacious, with a strong work ethic. I can carry heavy burdens. I will do whatever it takes to make something happen and get stuff done. If there's a hill to climb, I'll climb it. If the path forward is unclear, I'll find one. I don't give up easily.

I'm also kind and loyal. I enjoy exuding warmth. I'll be the first person to smile and say hello to someone on the street. I like picking up the check. I like saying yes more than I say no. I'm the kind of person who assumes the best in others until proven otherwise; I don't want to be a pessimist or a skeptic. And I like to build relationships that last—although, if I'm honest, I'm better at this in my business life than I am in my personal one.

The Downside

Here's the rub: The gifts that I have been blessed with have also been double-edged swords in my life. They are my strengths and my weaknesses.

TWO SIDES OF GRATITUDE
(OR, LEARNING TO LOVE MY CRITTER BRAIN)

My core strengths were born out of trauma. They were patterns I created to survive a difficult, chaotic, and deeply flawed childhood, and they have shaped my life in profound ways. I've held onto them because they are familiar to me, even when they don't bring me joy. I repeat them even when what I want and need is something different.

I've learned to recognize this in large part thanks to my wonderful mentor, Christine Comaford. Christine is an extraordinarily accomplished person who focuses her work on neuroscience-based leadership, culture, and personal-growth coaching. As Christine says in her New York Times bestseller, *Smart Tribes: How Teams Become Brilliant Together:* "Our brains do an amazing and wonderful job, but they don't like change very much. ... The parts [of our brain] that exist to keep us safe have created elegant patterning based on one-trial learning."[1]

Christine calls these parts the "critter brain," comprised of two parts: the reptilian brain, the oldest and most primitive part of our brain, which is focused on survival, and the limbic system,

---

[1] Comaford, Christine. *Smart Tribes: How Teams Become Brilliant Together,* Penguin Group, 2013; p. 23.

which is the emotional center of the brain and where our fight-flight-or-freeze response is located.

"Once our critter brain has equated a particular phenomenon with safety or survival, it will continue to carry out that program. And it will do so as long as we're not dead, because it really doesn't care about our quality of life—it cares about survival."[2]

In other words, when our critter brain is running the show—called "Critter State"—we gravitate toward behaviors that are familiar and repeat the patterns that the critter brain believes keep us alive, even when they don't feel particularly good or are even detrimental for us.

The Backstory

I grew up in a childhood of chaos, constant change, abuse, and abandonment. I escaped from it by diving headlong into school. I always loved to read and learn, and I was good at it. School brought structure to my day even when life at home was tense, which it usually was.

---

[2] Ibid., p. 24.

TWO SIDES OF GRATITUDE
(OR, LEARNING TO LOVE MY CRITTER BRAIN)

My parents divorced dramatically when I was 10. My mother remarried a physical and verbal abuser who kept the family walking on eggshells daily. I adored my brilliant and magnetic father, who had a repeat pattern of undermining his own life with thoughtless forays into sex and drugs. I visited him in jail at age 12. At age 15, I watched him move to Arizona with his new wife (age 18) and leave my younger brother and me behind to fend for ourselves with a stepfather that my mother was either too scared or in too much denial to leave.

So, I chose school. Being an excellent student gave me a sense of identity. Getting good grades was the only way I knew to feel worthy. The lessons were a point of continuity even as the house and town and schoolmates changed. I also believed that school could be a way out of the life I knew. And it was a way to hide in my room, away from the chaos, with homework as an excuse.

Later in life, that escapism became workaholism. As an adult, I've escaped facing my feelings by throwing myself into work. I took on more than others, and I worked harder to get to the right answer, usually harder than I needed to. For a very long time—decades—I believed, deep down, that my only value was in how much work I could handle.

We moved every year or two when I was a child. I don't think there was really any good reason for it. We always lived in the same county within a 20-mile radius. But, living in the pre-cellphone era, we might as well have moved to a different state. Every year, it meant a new house or apartment, a new room, a new school, new teachers, and a new set of friends. I was perpetually "the new kid"—the outlier.

Thankfully, before I went into the 10th grade (the transition year between middle and high school in our new town), my mother put her foot down and said we would stay put at least until I graduated high school, and we did.

I stepped into a high school that was a fusion of two middle schools. So, even though everyone had friends, they were meeting new kids left and right. For the first time, I was just another newbie. I made friends.

But things at home were worse than ever. My stepfather's abuse and instability had escalated. There were fights and blow-ups, and lines crossed that my little brother and I shouldn't have had to experience. During one epic rager, I fainted and hit my head so badly that I had a debilitating concussion. I missed weeks

TWO SIDES OF GRATITUDE
(OR, LEARNING TO LOVE MY CRITTER BRAIN)

of school and don't really remember much from that traumatic period. My grades dropped, and I graduated high school with some letters on my report card I had never seen before.

In retrospect, I was traumatized and depressed. Life at home was a nightmare, and I didn't have anybody to talk to. I had worked so hard to go to college, but while all my friends were moving into their dorms, I was told I would have to live at home. And I'd have to study something "practical" if I wanted to go at all. Once again, I was the outlier. So, I found myself enrolled in engineering school at Rutgers University and commuting. I was overwhelmed and alone. My first foray into higher education lasted a week. I went to work at the mall instead.

I was always the good kid. But that summer, I started to rebel. I had never been allowed to date and was only allowed to go to prom when my mom put her foot down for the second time. I developed a relationship with a secret boyfriend who was about three years older than I was. One weekend, my parents went away with my little brother. I had to work. So, the fraught decision was made to let me stay at home. By myself. For the first time ever.

On Saturday evening, I left work and spent an hour or two with my boyfriend. I walked into the house not late—probably around 8 pm—to a phone ringing off the hook.

"Hello?"

It was my stepfather. "I have been calling for hours. You were supposed to come home right after work. You don't know whether I'm two miles away or 200. When I get home, I'm going to kill you."

When I get home, I'm going to kill you.

So, I packed a single bag and left. I had been 18 years old for less than a week. I went into hiding for a few days and then moved to Lake Worth, Florida, with my boyfriend, where he was able to land a quick transfer with his job.

Once we got there, I went to the mall and bought an interview outfit: a green-and-black plaid skirt and matching top. Within a week, I went on an interview and got a job as a personal lines insurance underwriter, complete with on-the-job training.

The relationship didn't last. But the independence did.

TWO SIDES OF GRATITUDE
(OR, LEARNING TO LOVE MY CRITTER BRAIN)

I learned how to survive on my own. Within a year, I was in Los Angeles, living with a roommate in a real apartment, working a real job, and paying my own rent. I made friends, built a life, and made my way into the music business.

The one thing I didn't do? Reckon with what I'd been through. I tamped it down and forged ahead.

When I was 22, I got married. I'm sure I was not mature enough for marriage, but, in retrospect, I was desperately seeking family. He was also a forgotten child of divorce from a chaotic family—differently chaotic than mine, but my reptilian brain liked the vibe.

My new husband and I moved to Phoenix, Arizona, where I went to college at Arizona State, got a degree in history, and graduated from the university's Honors College. I was older than all the other undergrads (yup, the outlier), but I loved being in school again.

Upon graduation, I got a Ph.D. fellowship at Columbia University, so we moved to New York City. Growing up 25 miles outside of the Big Apple, it had always been a dream of mine to live there.

I felt out of place in graduate school. It was not a good fit, and I felt like an imposter among my classmates. After my first year, I took my master's degree and left. On to the next thing.

I got a job in travel publishing for *Frommer's Travel Guides*, which I loved. It tapped into my love of travel and my passion for research. I was good at it and felt at home there. It's also where I discovered my passion for building brands: What did it mean to build a common platform, a mission, and a belief system that could then be disseminated across 75 writers around the world, writing 200 book titles a year? It was a challenge that lit me up. In my four years there, I also built a new branded travel guide series for *Travel + Leisure* magazine, for the *...for Dummies* instructional series, and I wrote my first-ever travel guide to Hawaii.

I then jumped from my staff job to full-time freelance writing for Frommer's and other guidebooks and magazines. After 9/11, I decided to go to business school at Cornell University, four hours away from my husband and our home in Brooklyn. Once

TWO SIDES OF GRATITUDE
(OR, LEARNING TO LOVE MY CRITTER BRAIN)

I graduated, I got a job offer at a branding agency in Scottsdale, Arizona, that I couldn't resist, and we picked up and moved back to Phoenix. Fast-forward five more years, and I had the opportunity to jump ship and start my own branding agency in Colorado. That was the start of the business I now wholly own today—and the demise of my first marriage.

I could justify all these changes in my life. I had a keen desire to make something of myself. I was adventurous, welcomed a new challenge, and unafraid of change. All the changes made sense and were leading me somewhere.

Those things were true. But what was also true: In my ability to survive, I had recreated my own history of instability. If I blew up my life before others could, I remained in control. If I abandoned a person or a situation first, they couldn't abandon me.

So that's what I did, even if there was collateral damage along the way.

In my own business, I did great work but partnered poorly. I sought approval and acceptance from male partners who did not serve me well. When my business blew up in 2015 due to a merger that shouldn't have ever been forged (a story for another day), I found myself with no partners, a payroll of close to ten people, and just a few valuable contracts.

So, I rebuilt the business. But not without welcoming in yet another male partner, who I now refer to as my "rebound partner"—he told me I was smart and worthy at my most vulnerable time. Even though I had the processes and the people and the contracts, I gave him half the business. I was *that* desperate to be wanted, valued, and protected.

Two years later, I found evidence that he had been working on another venture. It turns out that you're not allowed to hide a side hustle from your business partner, especially if you're working on it on company time, using company resources, and you're trying to sell the output of the side hustle to company clients. This time, with the help of an amazing lawyer, I acted fast and saved the company.

And this time, I listened to Christine. She said, "Stop thinking you need a partner. You are strong enough to do this on your own."

TWO SIDES OF GRATITUDE
(OR, LEARNING TO LOVE MY CRITTER BRAIN)

So, I did.

The Reconciliation

The opposite of the Critter State is the Smart State.

When we're in Smart State, we're able to move beyond our most basic brain functions and take advantage of our highly evolved prefrontal cortex, where we make plans, solve complex problems, get creative, innovate, emotionally engage, think abstract thoughts, and have visionary ideas. We're able to recognize the difference between mere survival and what's actually good for us—and act accordingly. In Christine Comaford's words, "[In] Smart State, we have easy access to all of our resources and can respond from choice."[3]

I wish I could tell you that sometime around 2017, I made a permanent shift from Critter State to Smart State. If I did, I would be lying.

My experience is that my critter brain and my smart brain are not black and white; they're not a switch to be flipped. Instead,

---

[3] Ibid., page 25.

they're two ends of a continuum that I move along. I always have, but now I do so with a level of understanding, self-awareness, self-appreciation, forgiveness, and gratitude.

I continue to embrace change and am adept at adjusting to new circumstances. The pandemic demanded a serious pivot in my business, and I was able to tap into my deep well of experience to make it happen. But now I know the difference between smart shifts and critter-driven change. I recognize what change makes sense (versus change for change's sake) and make more well-informed and balanced choices.

I've gotten better at articulating and asking for what I need instead of running from what's not working. I say what I need to feel safe rather than retreating to old, subconsciously self-protective ways.

I'm finding empowerment in self-awareness. I'm redefining what success looks like for me. I've learned that freedom is my ultimate measure of success, and health and creativity are my ultimate sources of joy. I'm charting a path forward with more freedom in it to pursue the things I love outside of work. I still adore my work, but I want to be free to do more of the things I

TWO SIDES OF GRATITUDE
(OR, LEARNING TO LOVE MY CRITTER BRAIN)

love beyond it, to try new things, and to simply have more fun both in my work and outside of it.

I no longer define myself by the weight of what I can carry, nor do I allow others to define my worth that way. I find joy and reward in—and know the value and quality of—what I do. As a result, I'm finding that I serve my clients better than I ever have. When I don't live in fear of disapproval or rejection, I'm much better at being candid. I'm happier, and they are, too.

Now, in my 50s, I'm embracing my age and life stage. I'm not letting go of that hurt, damaged, smart, stoic little survivalist I once was. Instead, I'm working on giving her all the love, recognition, and power she deserves.

I acknowledge her strength, her skills, her joy, and her beauty.

I help her to feel safe in ways that recognize and value the dual nature of her gifts.

I forgive her for the errors she's made by acknowledging the exceptional growth that has resulted from undeserved hardship.

I empower her through self-awareness and build her confidence in the extraordinary toolkit she's developed along a winding, often difficult, and ultimately triumphant journey.

I recognize her victories in reinventing critter patterns as smart choices.

And I celebrate her independence and embrace the outlier within. Together we're standing out, not trying to blend in.

I can give her that. And for that, I'm grateful.

TWO SIDES OF GRATITUDE
(OR, LEARNING TO LOVE MY CRITTER BRAIN)

About the Author

Cheryl Farr is expert at creating and activating brands people love. She is Chief Strategist at SIGNAL Brand Innovation, a brand consultancy she founded in 2009 to help organizations align their vision, mission, team culture, and brand story with their business strategy to take their next great leap forward.

She empowers C-suite leaders to solve leadership challenges and identify game-changing, market-leading opportunities through brand strategy. She's on a mission to embed brand thinking into the growth-minded operating system of every organization to create brands that win.

Cheryl has worked with more than 100 emerging, established, and global brands, including Fairmont Hotels & Resorts, where she helped position the brand for expansive worldwide growth; Pulte Group, where she led the creation of a new consumer trending methodology to guide product and marketing innovations for the nation's largest homebuilder; PetSmart, where she led the sensory branding work that innovated the total in-store experience; and Cornell Hotel Society, where she crafted the ultimate rallying cry for the world's largest and most influential hospitality alumni network.

Cheryl is a former travel writer and editor for such brands as Frommer's, For Dummies, and Travel + Leisure. She holds graduate degrees from Cornell and Columbia universities and is a prolific writer and public speaker. She's also a passionate Midcentury modernist, Orangetheory fitness fanatic, long-suffering New York Giants fan, and dog mom to her talkative shih tzu, Harry Carson (@harrycarsonspeaks). She was named 2022 Enterprising Woman of the Year by Louisville Business First. She lives in Palm Springs, California.

TWO SIDES OF GRATITUDE
(OR, LEARNING TO LOVE MY CRITTER BRAIN)

Connect with Cheryl:

Visit SIGNAL Brand Innovation at www.signalbrand.co.

Email: cheryl@signalbrand.co

LinkedIn: www.linkedin.com/in/cherylannfarr/

Epilogue

"Sometimes the bad things that happen in our lives put us directly on the path to the most wonderful things that will ever happen to us."
—**Nicole Reed**

LIFE HAS A WAY OF TEACHING us its most profound lessons through our greatest challenges. As I reflect on the stories shared in these pages, I'm struck by how often what initially seemed like setbacks became catalysts for transformation. From medical crises to professional obstacles, from personal losses to moments of deep uncertainty, each challenge carried within it the seed of something extraordinary.

The women who contributed to this book understand this truth deeply. They've shown us how grateful leadership isn't about maintaining a forced smile through difficult times. Rather, it's about finding meaning in our struggles, strength in our vulnerability, and wisdom in our wounds. Their stories remind us that gratitude isn't just a practice for good times—it's a powerful force that can transform our darkest moments into opportunities for growth and connection.

I think about that Thanksgiving night in the ambulance with my brother Ryan, when the sound of a defibrillator changed everything I thought I knew about gratitude. I think about the years of infertility treatments that led to the perfect timing for adopting our beautiful boys. I think about watching our house burn down and discovering that what truly matters can never be destroyed. Each of these moments taught me that grateful leadership isn't about denying our challenges—it's about embracing them as part of our journey.

The Lead Like a Woman Show podcast and The *Lead Like a Woman* series of books continue to evolve and grow, reaching more women across the globe with each passing year. Through these platforms, we're creating spaces where women can share their stories of resilience, transformation, and grateful leadership. We're building a community where vulnerability is seen as strength, where challenges are viewed as opportunities, and where gratitude becomes a powerful force for positive change.

The journey toward grateful leadership is ongoing. Every day brings new opportunities to choose gratitude, to find meaning in our challenges, and to lead with an open heart. While we still have far to go in creating a more equitable world, every grateful leader who emerges from adversity stronger and more compassionate brings us closer to that goal.

I'm proud to Lead Like a Woman. I'm proud to lead with gratitude. I hope you are too.

See you soon!

Book Club Questions

SOME OF THE MOST IMPACTFUL DISCUSSIONS I have ever had have been around a table or a friend's living room while sipping beverages and eating snacks with other women. *Lead Like a Woman: GRATEFUL* is perfect for such a discussion!

The best book clubs encourage all voices to participate. Gather everyone in a large space and have a blast discussing everyone's thoughts and experiences with the book. Use the following questions to inspire conversation.

1. Were any of the stories in the book surprising? Which ones and why?

2. What did you find most inspiring about this book?

3. What was your biggest takeaway from the book?

4. What is the most important piece of advice offered in this book?

5. Who would you recommend this book to and why?

6. Which story or stories resonated with you the most? What made them particularly meaningful?

7. How has reading these stories changed your perspective on gratitude in leadership?

8. What challenges in your own life have unexpectedly led to growth or positive change?

9. What does grateful leadership mean to you? How has this definition evolved after reading the book?

10. What practices from the book do you plan to incorporate into your own leadership journey?

EPILOGUE

11. How do you think practicing gratitude can transform difficult situations in professional settings?

12. If you could ask one of the authors a question about grateful leadership, what would you ask and why?

13. What role do you think gratitude plays in creating more inclusive and supportive workplaces?

14. How has this book influenced your approach to handling challenges and setbacks?

Made in the USA
Monee, IL
09 March 2025